OLD TESTAMENT MESSAGE

A Biblical-Theological Commentary

Carroll Stuhlmueller, C.P. and Martin McNamara, M.S.C.

EDITORS

Old Testament Message, Volume 4

DEUTERONOMY

with an
Excursus on Covenant and Law

Richard Clifford, S.J.

Michael Glazier, Inc.
Wilmington, Delaware

First published in 1982 by:
MICHAEL GLAZIER, INC.
1723 Delaware Avenue
Wilmington, Delaware 19806

Distributed outside U.S., Canada & Philippines by:
GILL & MACMILLAN, LTD.
Goldenbridge, Inchicore
Dublin 8 Ireland

Library of Congress Catalog Card Number: 82-81222
International Standard Book Number
  Old Testament Message series: 0-89453-235-9
  Deuteronomy
  0-89453-239-1 (Michael Glazier, Inc.)
  7171-1168-7 (Gill & Macmillan, Ltd.)

Cover design by Lillian Brulc

Printed in the United States of America

CONTENTS

vi

Editors' Preface

Old Testament Message brings into our life and religion today the ancient word of God to Israel. This word, according to the book of the prophet Isaiah, had soaked the earth like "rain and snow coming gently down from heaven" and had returned to God fruitfully in all forms of human life (Isa 55:10). The authors of this series remain true to this ancient Israelite heritage and draw us into the home, the temple and the marketplace of God's chosen people. Although they rely upon the tools of modern scholarship to uncover the distant places and culture of the biblical world, yet they also refocus these insights in a language clear and understandable for any interested reader today. They enable us, even if this be our first acquaintance with the Old Testament, to become sister and brother, or at least good neighbor, to our religious ancestors. In this way we begin to hear God's word ever more forcefully in our own times and across our world, within our prayer and worship, in our secular needs and perplexing problems.

Because life is complex and our world includes, at times in a single large city, vastly different styles of living, we have much to learn from the Israelite Scriptures. The Old Testament spans forty-six biblical books and almost nineteen hundred years of life. It extends through desert, agricultural and urban ways of human existence. The literary style embraces a world of literature and human emotions. Its history began with Moses and the birth-pangs of a new people, it came of age politically and economically under David and Solomon, it reeled under the fiery threats of prophets like Amos and Jeremiah. The people despaired and yet were re-created with new hope during the Babylonian exile. Later reconstruction in the homeland and then the trauma of apocalyptic movements prepared for the revelation of "the mystery hidden for ages in God who created all things" (Eph 3:9).

While the Old Testament telescopes twelve to nineteen hundred years of human existence within the small country of Israel, any single moment of time today witnesses to the reenactment of this entire history across the wide expanse of planet earth. Each verse of the Old Testament is being relived somewhere in our world today. We need, therefore, the *entire* Old Testament and all twenty-three volumes of this new set, in order to be totally a "Bible person" within today's widely diverse society.

The subtitle of this series—"A Biblical-Theological Commentary"—clarifies what these twenty-three volumes intend to do.

Their *purpose* is theological: to feel the pulse of God's word for its *religious* impact and direction.

Their *method* is biblical: to establish the scriptural word firmly within the life and culture of ancient Israel.

Their *style* is commentary: not to explain verse by verse but to follow a presentation of the message that is easily understandable to any serious reader, even if this person is untrained in ancient history and biblical languages.

Old Testament Message—like its predecessor, *New Testament Message*—is aimed at the entire English-speaking world and so is a collaborative effort of an international team. The twenty-one contributors are women and men drawn from North America, Ireland, Britain and Australia. They are scholars who have published in scientific journals, but they have been chosen equally as well for their proven ability to communicate on a popular level. This twenty-three book set comes from Roman Catholic writers, yet, like the Bible itself, it reaches beyond interpretations restricted to an individual church and so enables men and women rooted in biblical faith to unite and so to appreciate their own traditions more fully and more adequately.

Most of all, through the word of God, we seek the blessedness and joy of those

who walk in the law of the Lord!...

who seek God with their whole heart (Ps. 119:1-2).

Carroll Stuhlmueller, C.P.   Martin McNamara, M.S.C.

INTRODUCTION

IN NO BOOK of the Bible is exclusive fidelity to the Lord held up so insistently to Israel as it is in Deuteronomy. Moses speaks throughout, addressing the people on the threshold of the Lord's land on how they are to live as befits people rescued from Egypt. Israel's essence as a people, ever receiving the life-giving land, ever hearing the word of God through Moses, is unforgettably expressed. As noble as is the theme, however, readers unaware of the covenant background and rhetoric of the book are unlikely to be moved, and may even find the speeches repetitive and monotonous. To appreciate the freshness and power of the sermons, one must first understand how the book came to be organized into its present thirty-four chapters and how covenant traditions were shaped into perennially moving sermons.

I. Stages of Composition.

The process that led to the present shape of Deuteronomy took nearly 200 years, from the mid-eighth to the mid-sixth centuries (certain parts of the book are even older). This commentary proposes modestly, in the face of conflicting scholarly theories, that the formation process took place in three principal stages. In the first stage, Deut

1:1-3:28 + 31:1-8 served as the preface to a single historical work stretching from Joshua to 2 Kings. Modern scholars call this history the Deuteronomic or Deuteronomistic History (DH). This commentary uses the latter term "Deuteronomistic" for the History and reserves the adjective "Deuteronomic" for the book of Deuteronomy. It is generally agreed that DH was composed in the latter part of King Josiah's reign (640-609 B.C.) as part of the royal program of reform and territorial expansion. The editor or redactor of DH, who is sometimes abbreviated Dtr¹ (= first redactor of Deuteronomy and DH), brought together a variety of old traditions, combining them with some of his own material, in order to illustrate how Israel prospered in the land to the degree in which it lived according to the word of the Lord. That word was expressed in the Mosaic law and in the Davidic promise.

The second stage was the reediting of DH during the Exile in the sixth century, about fifty or sixty years after the first edition. Not long after the publication of the first edition, King Josiah had been killed in battle (609 B.C.), Judah depopulated, and its capitol, Jerusalem, destroyed (587 B.C.). Such catastrophes forced revision of the optimism of Josiah's reign. 2 Kgs 23:25 has the look of the original ending with Josiah as the divinely blessed Davidide; it shows no awareness of his inglorious death. The immediately following material in 2 Kgs 23:26-25:30 looks like an update of ca. 560 B.C.; 2 Kgs 25:27-30 is the last datable event in DH, and took place in 562 B.C. The exilic redactor, conventionally Dtr², not only added material to the ending of DH; he inserted considerable material to its beginning. Into the old preface to DH (Deut 1:1-3:28 + 31:1-8), Dtr² inserted the lengthy speech of 4:44-28:68. He framed this speech with two other speeches, 4:1-40 at the beginning and 29:1-32:47 at the end. The two framing speeches were designed to relate the central speech and indeed the whole of DH to exilic concerns.

The great speech of 4:44—28:68, a venerable document at the time of its insertion, is generally thought by scholars to be the document found in the temple in 621 B.C. that inspired aspects of the Josianic reform (2 Kings 23). It is probable that Dtr[2] also imposed the four-fold division of the book to guide the reader through the complexity of the newly augmented book: "these are the words" in 1:1 introduces the first section 1:1-4:43; "this is the law" in 4:44 introduces the second section 4:44-28:68; "these are the words" in 29:1, the third section 29:1-32:52; and "this is the blessing" in 33:1, the fourth section 33:1-34:12.

In the third and final stage, the Priestly redactor (P), responsible also for the exilic reshaping of old traditions to form the tetrateuch (four books) of Genesis-Numbers, made Deuteronomy the fifth book of the Pentateuch (five books) by making the traditional account of the death of Moses the final chapter of Deuteronomy. P's aim in making the former preface to DH the fifth book of the Pentateuch was apparently to isolate the period of Moses and of the law as a separate entity to guide Israel restored from the Exile.

II. Literary Form.

Structure is only one clue to a piece of literature; a second clue is the genre, the type of literature of which it is an instance. Though Deuteronomy is often described as a law book, it is in reality a series of speeches of Moses. The law of the speeches is different from modern conceptions of Anglo-Saxon law. See the excursus on Law and Covenant. The sophisticated rhetoric of the speeches—how they develop ideas in order to persuade the hearer to a particular course of action—will be noted in the commentary under the individual speeches. The genre of much of the book (chaps. 4-30) can be fixed even more precisely than simply "speech"; it is speech modeled on the covenant formulary.

Covenant formulary is a term given by modern scholars to the pattern discernible in West Semitic treaties of the second and first millennium B.C. Examples of second millennium treaties are those used by the Hittite Empire (1450-1200 B.C.) for keeping their borders secure and for maintaining control over subordinate states. The essentials, which never varied, were the promulgation of the obligations assumed, and the invocation of the gods with the implication of divine sanctions. Nearly always there were more elements. The following is a typical scheme.

> Titulary.
> History of the relationship between the two kings, usually in precise, accurate detail, and in personal terms.
> Statement of relationship, i.e. the general statement of the unity which is to exist between the vassal and his lord, e.g. "thou, Niqmepa, and thy country are my servants, and thou shalt be faithful to the king of the land of Hatti . . . and as thou thyself, thy wife, thy people and thy land are dear to thee so shall . . . Hatti be dear to thee."
> Stipulations.
> List of divine witnesses.
> Curses and blessings.

The covenant formulary persisted as a genre well into the first millennium. The Neo-Assyrian Empire (935-612 B.C.) used it as a diplomatic instrument in its imperialist policy. The traditional stipulations, invocation of the gods, and curses always appear, though not always in the traditional order. The curses are emphasized in these later treaties, elaborated beyond the sober Hittite formulary. Recent studies suggest the covenant formulary used in the Empire's diplomacy with such western client states as Tyre and Qedar is really a West Semitic institution borrowed by the Assyrians. It was thus a legal institution entirely familiar in all its elements to the Israelites.

The covenant formulary inspired the organization of the central speech of Deut 4:44—28:68, and, less directly, 4:1-40 and 29:1—30:20.

Setting of the scene for a treaty turned into a
  speech. 4:44-49
Historical prologue interspersed with exhortation.
  Chaps. 5-11
Stipulations. 12:1-26:15
Invocation—adjuration. 26:16-19
Blessings and curses. 28:1-68

Deuteronomy is not itself a covenant formulary. Covenant formulary properly is the record of a liturgical ceremony held before the witnessing gods detailing the legal
relationship between one king and another, a suzerain and a
vassal. Deut 4:44—28:68 turns the legal institution into a
speech that is designed to persuade Israel to see in Yahweh
its only sovereign. In the formulary tradition the suzerain
often told the history of his own and his father's relationship
to the vassal king, emphasizing his kindness and specific
benefits, in order to move the vassal to grateful obedience to
the stipulations. Relations between nations were personalized in the relations between the kings who embody their
nations. It was not "a government of laws, not men"; quite
the contrary! From such personalism arises the insistence in
the treaties on virtues such as loyalty and love and on terms
such as "my brother" in the kings' address to each other. In
chaps. 5-11, the history of the relationship that is found in
the covenant formulary is adapted by the Israelite author
into sermons on loyalty to Yahweh alone. Historical remin-
iscense is combined with exhortation in order to persuade.

III. Date.

What is the date and what are the circumstances that
may have given rise to the great document of 4:44—28:68?
Until recently the prevailing view was that the chapters
recorded the preaching of country priests in northern Israel
who spoke vividly the demands of the Mosaic covenant.
When the North fell in 722, the sermonic traditions were
supposedly brought south to Judah and in time became the

text of King Josiah's reform beginning in 621 B.C. Several recent scholars, impressed by the newly published Neo-Assyrian treaties and by the likelihood of Jerusalem as the place of composition, propose that the main Deuteronomic traditions were given their shape in the face of the Neo-Assyrian threat to Israel's existence in the late eighth century, probably under King Hezekiah (715-687 B.C.). Judah, forced like other small West Semitic states to deal with the Neo-Assyrian superpower through the legal instruments of the covenant formulary, was stirred to rethink its relationship to its Lord by means of the same formulary. Israel of course had always had a covenant with Yahweh but not one worked out through a covenant formulary. In the Neo-Assyrian crisis Israel took the very instrument of imperialism and made it the instrument of a powerful new theology. The new formulation in 4:44-28:68 was so compelling that it inspired later sermons like Deut 4:1-40 and 29:1-30:20. It also animated the reform of Josiah a century later.

IV. Religious Message Today.

What is the theological significance of Deuteronomy for today? First, it is the book of Moses; he is the law mediator for every generation of Israel. The text is at pains to state that his office as lawspeaker is handed on to his successors, first to Joshua, and then to others (Deut 3:28; 5:1—6:3; 18:15-22; 31:1-29). The transferability of the Mosaic function is the reason why sermons written in the eighth or sixth centuries can be attributed to Moses. Whoever holds the office of lawspeaker stands in the place of Moses for his generation and can preach *in persona Moysis* (in the person of Moses).

A recurring emphasis of the preaching is loyalty to Yahweh alone in preference to the gods whom Israel will be tempted to serve in the land. Israel has seen the saving power of Yahweh in Egypt and in the wilderness journey;

now it must learn to see the divine power in a different arena—the land which the Lord gives them. The land is the sphere which discloses Yahweh. Israel is invited to see Yahweh as the God who gives life in the land. Where Israel struggles to be loyal to the Lord alone, amid competing claims upon its heart and mind, Moses will continue to speak the words which give life.

A note on the use of this book. Because of insufficient space, it was not possible to reprint the entire text of Deuteronomy. The excerpts have been selected to provide the reader with a thread through dense material or with a sample of the rest of the text. The reader is advised to read the entire biblical text in an unabridged Bible both before and after reading the commentary.

THE FIRST SPEECH. 1:1—4:43

Section 1.
The Lord's Word Guides Israel to the
Threshold of the Land
1:1—3:29

PREFACE TO THE BOOK OF DEUTERONOMY AND TO THE FIRST SPEECH. 1:1-5.

1 These are the words that Moses spoke to all Israel beyond the Jordan in the wilderness, in the Arabah over against Suph, between Paran and Tophel, Laban, Hazeroth, and Dizahab. ²It is eleven days' journey from Horeb by the way of Mount Seir to Kadesh-barnea. ³And in the fortieth year, on the first day of the eleventh month, Moses spoke to the people of Israel according to all that the Lord had given him in commandment to them, ⁴after he had defeated Sihon the king of the Amorites, who lived in Heshbon, and Og the king of Bashan, who lived in Ashtaroth and in Edrei. ⁵Beyond the Jordan, in the land of Moab, Moses undertook to explain this law, saying,

The several editings of the Deuteronomic traditions before their final arrangement in the present book are reflected in these verses which introduce not only the speeches of Moses in chaps. 1-3 + 31 and chap. 4, but the entire book as well. As already noted, the four-fold arrangement of the book is signaled by alternating introductions, "these are the words," in 1:1; "this is the law *(torah)*" in 4:44; "these are the words (of the covenant)" in 29:1; and "this is the blessing" in 33:1. The first section of Deuteronomy, 1:1—4:43, begins with "These are the words."

The stringing together of regional names in v. 1b, from "in the wilderness" to "Di-Zahab" has never been satisfactorily explained, chiefly because the places cannot be located on a map with any certainty. Are they sites in Transjordan within the general area called "Beyond-the-Jordan" of v. 1a, or are they a sample of the sites visited earlier in the journey meant to inform the reader that the book records the words of Moses not only in Transjordan but in all previous stages of the journey? No decisive answer is possible. Verses 2 and 3 are generally regarded by scholars as later insertions. They are of course part of the canonical text. The former verse gives the length of the journey from Horeb, the sacred mountain of revelation, to Kadesh-barnea, the first station to be mentioned in this speech (1:19-46). The eleven days may reflect the length of time it took ancient pilgrims to visit the site of Horeb, a pilgrimage practice that is suggested in the story of the prophet Elijah in the ninth century (1 Kings 19). A tradition going back to Byzantine times identifies Horeb/Sinai with the impressive mountain Jebel Musa in the Sinai Peninsula. Ancient biblical poetry, however, suggests that the mountain was directly south of Canaan and speaks impressively of his advance with an army from the south. "The Lord came from Sinai, / and dawned from Seir upon us; / he shone forth from Mount Paran, / he came from the ten thousands of holy ones, / with flaming fire at his right hand." (Deut 33:2 and cf. Judg 5:4; Ps 68:7-8; Hab 3:3). The second insertion, v. 3, is from the Priestly Source (P) which characteristically interprets the wilderness journey as a procession regulated by a liturgical calendar. The next new date after v. 3 is also P, Josh 4:19: "The people came up out of the Jordan on the tenth day of the first month [of the following year], and they encamped in Gilgal on the eastern borders of Jericho.'' Thus according to Josh 4:19 and the other notices in the calendar series of P (Exod 12:3, 6, 41, 51; 16:1; 40:1f.; Num 1:1; 9:11; 10:11; 33:38), Moses' addresses in Deuteronomy are the last liturgical events of the wilderness period. Moses dies on the very day he addresses Israel according to Deut 32:48. A new calendar begins in Canaan under Joshua according to Josh 4:19—5:12. The P date notice is then a reminder that Moses' speech ends the wilderness period and constitutes a final great attempt to relate the traditions of the exodus and wilderness period to the new situation of life upon the land.

Verses 4-5, which speak of the defeat of the two Transjordanian kings Sihon and Og, are directly prefatory to chaps. 1-3 and show us that Moses is not only to be reckoned as lawgiver but also as successful leader of his people in war. ''This law *(torah)''* is broader in Hebrew than in English. It means authoritative national tradition both narrative and legal, the same meaning that it has in Ps 78:1-4 and elsewhere in the Bible.

EXCURSUS ON THE SPEECH
CHAPS. 1—3; 31.

Perhaps only in an oral culture like Israel's where people remembered their national traditions accurately and with ready emotional recall on the one hand, and on the other expected their liturgical speakers to recast those traditions freely, can this lengthy speech of Moses be fully appreciated. Modern public speakers generally figure out ahead of time what ''point'' they wish to make, summarizing it for themselves as an abstract proposition. They then illustrate their ''point'' with ''stories.'' The ancient speaker let the story itself carry the meaning, selecting or omitting details within a narrative outline essentially familiar to the hearers or readers. With no wish to say that the narrative mode is childish, one may suggest the Israelite attitude toward their stories was like that of adults who have not had their childhood instinct for narrative driven out of them. Children frequently ask that a familiar story be told to them, not because they don't know the story or its ending, but because they are fascinated with the details and variations that the teller will introduce.

To the modern reader familiar only in a general way with Israel's traditions, the long narrative in chaps. 1-3 may seem maddeningly repetitious of what has been read already in Exodus and Numbers. For example, the story of the spies and the subsequent attacks in 1:19-46 is found also in Numbers 13-14. The installation of judges in 1:9-18 is found in Exodus 18. What need is there to tell the story again if the public is already familiar with it? The Israelite hearer, respectful more than we of narrative as a source of truth rather than an illustration of a proposition, would not have focused on the repetition of details but on the new story that emerged from those details. In chaps. 1-3, Moses retells the journey of Israel from Horeb to the Trans-jordanian staging area for crossing the Jordan, selecting only those details that make his point. His point: only when Israel follows the word of the Lord mediated through Moses (or "a prophet like Moses") can they possess the land. When they disobey and follow their own will, the Lord will turn his holy war against them instead of their enemies. When they obey he is with them in his power.

The long speech is virtually all narrative, a review of the past forty years of the people's variegated response to the word of the Lord. The unity of the speech has not always been seen by commentators who have been insensitive to the Hebrew tradition of oratory. The best proof that the speech is unified is to show that it "works" as as narrative, that the details fit within a single story line. For fine points one will have to consult the commentary under the in-dividual sections, but a précis will make a preliminary case for unity.

The speech of Moses begins with the quotation of the divine command, uttered at Horeb, to invade the land (1:6-8). On the way to Kadesh-barnea in the south, which was the most direct and logical starting area, Moses appoints judges to help him in his governance of the people. The very number of the people, a result of divine blessing, has created the need for Moses to share his authority (1:9-18). It is a prelude to the sharing of his authority with Joshua in time to come. The people's disobedience to the divine command provokes a divine oath that none of the evil generation shall enter except Caleb and Joshua (1:18-46). During Israel's forced wait of forty years until the rebellious generation died out, they saw evidence of the Lord's settling of kindred people in neighboring lands, the children of Esau in Seir and the children of Lot in Moab (2:1-15). With the rebels out of the way, the holy war for the land can now resume, first against Sihon the Amorite (2:16-37) and then against Og king of Bashan (3:1-11). The victory won, Moses can now distribute the lands of the Transjordan to the tribes of Reuben, Gad, and Manasseh (3:12-22). Moses, because he is too closely identified with the rebellious generation, cannot lead his people across the Jordan. He commissions Joshua, in the sight of all the people, to lead the people in war and distribute the land just as he had done in Transjordan (3:23-28 and 31:1-8).

ISRAEL'S REFUSAL TO INVADE BY THE SOUTHERN ROUTE LEADS TO AN ANTI-EXODUS AND ANTI-HOLY WAR
1:6-46.

> ⁶"The Lord our God said to us in Horeb, 'You have stayed long enough at this mountain; ⁷turn and take your journey, and go to the hill country of the Amorites, and to all their neighbors in the Arabah, in the hill country and in the lowland, and in the Negeb, and by the seacoast, the land of the Canaanites, and

Lebanon, as far as the great river, the river Euphrates. ⁸Behold, I have set the land before you; go in and take possession of the land which the Lord swore to your fathers, to Abraham, to Isaac, and to Jacob, to give to them and to their descendants after them.'

⁹"At that time I said to you, 'I am not able alone to bear you; ¹⁰the Lord your God has multiplied you, and behold, you are this day as the stars of heaven for multitude. ¹¹May the Lord, the God of your fathers, make you a thousand times as many as you are, and bless you, as he has promised you! ¹²How can I bear alone the weight and burden of you and your strife? ¹³Choose wise, understanding, and experienced men, according to your tribes, and I will appoint them as your heads.' ¹⁴And you answered me, 'The thing that you have spoken is good for us to do.'

²⁰"And I said to you, 'You have come to the hill country of the Amorites, which the Lord our God gives us. ²¹Behold, the Lord your God has set the land before you; go up, take possession, as the Lord, the God of your fathers, has told you; do not fear or be dismayed.' ²²Then all of you came near me, and said, 'Let us send men before us, that they may explore the land for us, and bring us word again of the way by which we must go up and the cities into which we shall come.'

²⁶"Yet you would not go up, but rebelled against the command of the Lord your God; ²⁷and you murmured in your tents, and said, 'Because the Lord hated us he has brought us forth out of the land of Egypt, to give us into the hand of the Amorites, to destroy us.

³⁴"And the Lord heard your words, and was angered, and he swore, ³⁵'Not one of these men of this evil generation shall see the good land which I swore to give to your fathers, ³⁶except Caleb the son of Jephunneh; he shall see it, and to him and to his children I will give the land upon which he has trodden, because he has wholly followed the Lord!' ³⁷The Lord was angry with me also on your account, and said, 'You also shall not

go in there; [38]Joshua the sun of Nun, who stands before
you, he shall enter; encourage him, for he shall cause
Israel to inherit it.

[41]"Then you answered me, 'We have sinned against
the Lord; we will go up and fight, just as the Lord our
God commanded us.' And every man of you girded on
his weapons of war, and thought it easy to go up into
the hill country. [42]And the Lord said to me, 'Say to
them, Do not go up or fight, for I am not in the midst of
you; lest you be defeated before your enemies.' [43]So I
spoke to you, and you would not hearken; but you
rebelled against the command of the Lord, and were
presumptuous and went up into the hill country. [44]Then
the Amorites who lived in that hill country came out
against you and chased you as bees do and beat you
down in Seir as far as Hormah. [45]And you returned and
wept before the Lord; but the Lord did not hearken to
your voice or give ear to you. [46]So you remained at
Kadesh many days, the days that you remained there."

The excerpts sketch the story line. Moses narrates how
Israel is told to leave Horeb and invade Canaan from the
southern site of Kadesh-barnea, refuses to attack, and by
divine oath the "evil generation (except for Caleb and
Joshua)" is forbidden to enter the land. Then in the face of
the oath, Israel tries to invade but is defeated.

The speech is a reworking of the old traditions undoubtedly familiar to hearers even before the reshaping
here. The appointment of legal assistants to Moses is
found in Exod 18:23-27; the disastrous episode of the
spies, in Numbers 13 and 14. One need not hold that
Deuteronomy uses as souces the old Pentateuchal traditions in their present form. Israel and other ancient peoples
treasured diversity in narrative and could embrace variant
versions.

The Deuteronomic imprint is strong amid the traditional
material. In Num 10:11-36 Israel leaves Sinai only when
the cloud leads them and they then follow the ark in stately

procession. In Deut 1:6-8 they are told directly by the Lord to leave Horeb and go to the hill country of the Amorites. From first to last in the speech Israel's movements are directed by the divine word originating at Horeb. The success or failure of the people in their quest for the land is directly proportionate to their obedience or disobedience to the word mediated by Moses. If they disobey, they are defeated by the native inhabitants (1:41-45). If they obey, they defeat the inhabitants (2:24—3:11) or at least are led safely through potentially hostile territory (2:8b-12, 16-23). Elsewhere in Deuteronomy the same phenomenon of obedience-success and disobedience-failure is described in the language of blessing and curse.

Verses 7-8 is a description of the Promised Land. The "hill country of the Amorites" is a frequent Deuteronomic designation for the Promised Land, called "Canaan" in other sources. The boundaries of the Promised Land presumed in the patriarchal stories and described in texts such as Num 34:1-12 and v. 7b conform to the boundaries of the the ancient Egyptian province of Canaan. The old province of "Canaan" did not include Transjordan but did extend far north, finally bulging northeast to touch the Euphrates River. Here the ideal boundaries are not depicted with the geographical exactness of Numbers 34, but through a piling up of regional designations. The promise to the "fathers," i.e., the patriarchs or ancestors, assumes a vast importance in Moses' speeches. It generally expresses the absolutely gratuitous gift of land to Abraham, Isaac, and Jacob and to their descendents, decided upon by the Lord centuries before the present generation.

The appointment of judges to help Moses is frequently seen by scholars as a late insertion, but it makes perfect sense in a speech that has as its chief concern how the Mosaic office is handed on to another, Joshua (cf. esp. 3:21, 28, and 31:1-8). At Horeb itself Moses shares his authority with wise representatives of the tribes chosen by the people themselves. The appointment is cast in an entirely positive light. The cause of the appointment of assistants is the wonderful increase in the number of people. The people, now like the stars for multitude in fulfillment of the promise to the patriarchs (Gen 15:5), is simply too huge for one man to govern. The fulfillment of the promise of progeny in these verses suggests that the promise of the land made to the patriarchs will soon be fulfilled as well. *RSV* "strife" in v. 12 ought to be translated "legal cases."

The vigorous freedom of the people is emphasized here (in contrast to Exod 18:13-27), an emphasis that one expects in homiletic literature designed to elicit free assent. Note also the role of the free assent of the people in the account of the spies, vv. 22-23, 27-28, 41.

Verses 19-46 describe the attack on the land from the south. Moses reminds the people of the sacred command in vv. 20-21. They ask, however, for a scouting report before attacking (v. 22). Comparison with Num 13:1 where the Lord, not the people, orders the spies suggests that the popular request actually arises from doubt. That doubt will grow into a rebellion.

When Moses tells the people, "Behold the Lord has set the land before you; go up . . . do not fear or be dismayed," he is playing the role of officer in a holy war. War in the ancient east was a sacral affair. The prestige and power of the patron god or gods of the warring nations was thought to be involved. In line with the general Eastern view that important earthly events and institutions mirrored and "re-presented" heavenly realities, earthly armies mirrored the heavenly prestige and power of their divine patrons. Since the really decisive struggle took place in the heavenly world between the gods, the earthly warriors had to find out beforehand if their own deity was powerful enough to bring victory to them. If they learned their deity was indeed going out to fight with them against their enemies' patron deities and was powerful that day, then they could charge into the fray with reckless courage knowing the enemy was "in their hand." We shall see below that all the booty after the victory belonged to the god, who after all was the true victor. It might have to be returned to the god through the practice of *herem,* or "devotion" to the sacred sphere. This theory lies behind the biblical practice of "utterly destroying" one's enemies, so disturbing to modern readers. Moses exhorts the troops to the reckless courage befitting warriors who know their god is fighting for them. Though the request for more intelligence in the heat of holy war exhortation seems a lukewarm response, Moses finds it reasonable.

The essence of the spies' report is favorable—it is a good land which the Lord gives (v. 25). Yet the message is mixed—a good land to be sure but defended by a fearsome people, the legendary Anakim. The people can only quote the spies' description of the difficulties. Moses cites only the great record of the divine warrior in Egypt and in the wilderness. They have seen his works with their own eyes. Why doubt his power now? This unpleasant dialogue between Moses and the people in vv. 26-33, in which the people move from simple rebellion to accusation that the Lord intends to destroy them, is suddenly quelled by the divine oath. It is the first speech of the Lord since the initial command to attack in vv. 6-8. The Lord swears that this evil generation will not see the land given to their ancestors except Caleb because of his faithful past and Joshua because of his future role as successor of Moses.

Moses is not to go in because of the people's sin! Deuteronomy records no personal sin of Moses. Only Priestly tradition, in Num 20:1-13, records such a sin. Moses is so identified with his people that he falls under the oath banning common entrance. Here at the beginning of Deuteronomy, Moses is portrayed as one denied entrance to the land because of sin. His words thereby gain in seriousness, and he becomes a most poignant speaker to Israel in Exile. He knows what it is like to be without a land. The servant who suffers for his people is not new in the Bible, whether it be First Isaiah's instinctive lament "how long" upon hearing judgment pronounced upon his

people in Isa 6:11, or Jeremiah "confessing," or the
mysterious servant freeing others by his suffering in Isa
52:13—53:12. All of these great servants of the Lord are
kin to Moses.

The folly of the people is not cured by their hearing the
divine oath. The horrible effect of the oath will become
clear only in the next chapter. The people continue to use
the freedom that led them to demand spies and to rebel;
they will decide on their own to invade, even if God disap-
proves (vv. 41-43). They had actually been told to go back
to the Red Sea and await a further word (v. 40). The
disobedience to the second divine command has predic-
table effects. They are roundly defeated since the Lord did
not go out as their heavenly warrior. The first scene of the
speech ends in fruitless mourning for dead comrades and
missed opportunities. It lasts a long time (v. 46).

WAITING FOR A NEW GENERATION TO ARISE
2:1-15

2 "Then we turned, and journeyed into the wilderness
in the direction of the Red Sea, as the Lord told me; and
for many days we went about Mount Seir. ²Then the
Lord said to me, ³"You have been going about this
mountain country long enough; turn northward. ⁴And
command the people, You are about to pass through the
territory of your brethren the sons of Esau, who live in
Seir; and they will be afraid of you. So take good heed;
⁵do not contend with them; for I will not give you any of
their land, no, not so much as for the sole of the foot to
tread on, because I have given Mount Seir to Esau as a
possession.

⁹"And the Lord said to me, 'Do not harass Moab or
contend with them in battle, for I will not give you any
of their land for a possession, because I have given Ar to
the sons of Lot for a possession.'

¹³" 'Now rise up, and go over the brook Zered.' So
we went over the brook Zered. ¹⁴And the time from our

leaving Kadesh-barnea until we crossed the brook Zered
was thirty-eight years, until the entire generation, that
is, the men of war, had perished from the camp, as the
Lord had sworn to them. ¹⁵For indeed the hand of the
Lord was against them, to destroy them from the camp,
until they had perished.''

Finally the people obeyed the command to retrace their
route, Moses recalls in his speech (1:40). They followed a
southeasterly route to the region northeast of the Gulf of
Aqaba, there to await a further word. The Lord gives a
command like his first, "You have been going about this
mountain country long enough; turn northward" (2:3; cf.
1:6-7). The people are to travel through the mountain
country of Seir on the eastern side of the Arabah and south
of the Dead Sea. Instead of invading, they are told to go
through Seir peacefully, avoiding any offence and provocation to war. For the land was given as a possession to
the children of Esau. They go through protected, as they
have been for the past forty years.

It is the assumption of the chapter that in patriarchal
times—the olden days of Abraham, Isaac, and Jacob, the
days also of Esau the less favored brother of Jacob, and
Lot the hapless nephew of Abraham—the Lord made a
decisive distribution of all the land in this part of the world.
At the same time that the Lord swore to "your fathers" to
give them the land, i.e., the hill country of the Amorites,
he also assigned adjacent land to their relatives. So the
children of Esau have their land as a "possession" (v. 5),
the same word used for Israel's land. A similar grant was
made to the children of Lot who were given Moab, the territory east of the Dead Sea between the Zered and the Arnon (v. 9), and the territory of the Ammonites (v. 19).
Verses 10-12 and 20-23 provide notes on the inhabitants of
the territories before the entry of the children of Esau and
Lot; these verses are generally considered late insertions.
Additions they may be, but they make perfect sense in the
perspective of the Lord's reassignment of lands and
peoples in patriarchal times. The text speaks of the old in-

habitants in legendary fashion. Little today is known of
the peoples bearing the names of Emim, Rephaim, etc. The
final element in the name, *-im,* is the plural in Hebrew. The
Rephaim (vv. 11, 20) are probably a warrior guild formed
of land-owning aristocracy rather than an ethnic group.
And it may well be that the other terms are similarly to be
understood. The important point is that those people,
mighty as they were at one time, have been dispossessed by
the Lord when he swore to give the land, the hill country of
the Amorites, to our fathers. The presence of the children
of Lot and of Esau in their allotted lands should assure
Israel that they will one day receive their possession as well,
given as it is by the Lord of all territories and peoples.

With the command in 2:13 to cross the brook Zered on
the southeast shore of the Dead Sea, Moses comes to the
turning point of his speech. The text is careful to say thirty-
eight years have elapsed, i.e., since the rebellion of
Kadesh-barnea and the Lord's oath that none of "this evil
generation shall see the good land" (v. 1:35). Forty years,
not thirty-eight, is the traditional time in the Bible for a
generation to pass away. Apparently the Deuteronomist
wanted to leave sufficient time in his chronology for the
later conquest of Heshbon and Bashan and the allotment
of land, described in chaps. 2 and 3. At any rate, the evil
generation is gone and the children of that generation can
now go in and possess it. Chapter 1 has prepared for this
day. The rebellious generation had claimed that their
children would become a prey in the land (1:39); the opposite has turned out to be true.

More importantly, as W. L. Moran has pointed out, the
oath of the Lord that none would enter of that generation
has proven to be literally fulfilled. The language of 2:14-16
shows that the Lord has come against his own people in
war, in an "anti-Exodus." Instead of attacking their
enemies, he attacked Israel, leaving not a warrior alive.
The war language used in these verses supports the shocking conclusion. The generation that perished is expressly
called "the men of war"; they perish "from the [military]

camp" (v. 14). "The hand of the Lord against . . . " is a term of war. Once again the power of the word of the Lord, uttered as an oath in 1:34-35, is experienced by the people.

ISRAEL FOLLOWS THE LORD VICTORIOUSLY IN TRANSJORDAN
2:16—3:11

²⁴" 'Rise up, take your journey, and go over the valley of the Arnon; behold, I have given into your hand Sihon the Amorite, king of Heshbon, and his land; begin to take possession, and contend with him in battle. ²⁵This day I will begin to put the dread and fear of you upon the peoples that are under the whole heaven, who shall hear the report of you and shall tremble and be in anguish because of you.'

²⁶"So I sent messengers from the wilderness of Kedemoth to Sihon the king of Heshbon, with words of peace, saying, ²⁷"Let me pass through your land; I will go only by the road, I will turn aside neither to the right nor to the left. ²⁸You shall sell me food for money, that I may eat, and give me water for money, that I may drink; only let me pass through on foot, ²⁹as the sons of Esau who live in Seir and the Moabites who live in Ar did for me, until I go over the Jordan into the land which the Lord our God gives to us.' ³⁰But Sihon the king of Heshbon would not let us pass by him; for the Lord your God hardened his spirit and made his heart obstinate, that he might give him into your hand, as at this day. ³¹And the Lord said to me, 'Behold, I have begun to give Sihon and his land over to you; begin to take possession, that you may occupy his land.' ³²Then Sihon came out against us, he and all his people, to battle Jahaz. ³³And the Lord our God gave him over to us; and we defeated him and his sons and all his people. ³⁴And we captured all his cities at that time and utterly

destroyed every city, men, women, and children; we left none remaining; [35]only the cattle we took as spoil for ourselves, with the booty of the cities which we captured. [36]From Ar´er, which is on the edge of the valley of the Arnon, and from the city that is in the valley, as far as Gilead, there was not a city too high for us; the Lord our God gave all into our hands. [37]Only to the land of the sons of Ammon you did not draw near, that is, to all the banks of the river Jabbok and the cities of the hill country, and wherever the Lord our God forbade us."

The excerpts, just quoted, from this section of the speech, make it clear that a new stage has begun. The rebellious generation whom the Lord swore would never see the land are gone, replaced by their children. "Today pass over the boundary of Moab at Ar." Probably Ar, the chief city of Moab, stands for Moab here through metonymy (part for the whole) as it does in v.9. Hence they are to pass through Moab, through Ar. The land of the Ammonites to the east is off-limits since the land had already been given to Lot for a possession. Verses 20-23, like vv. 10-12, describe the displacement of peoples in the great land reassignment in the time of the ancestors.

Verse 24, the command to cross the Arnon River, the border between Moab and the kingdom of Heshbon, is the true beginning of the war. The Lord speaks as a warrior, in the language of war. "I have given into your hand Sihon the Amorite, king of Heshbon, and his land" (v. 24). The panic that the Lord promises to send upon Israel's enemies is a standard weapon of ancient war. Battle was often decided quickly, involving relatively few troops. With no electronic communications and only primitive maps, armies were vulnerable to rumors and surprise attacks. Not a few battles were won by a smaller army using the tactics of surprise. See the story of Gideon and his hundred men in Judg 7:9-24. The fear of Israel's army under Moses that falls upon Transjordan will also fall upon Canaan when Joshua leads the Israelite army. The Bible itself will point out this parallel in Josh 2:9-11. Joshua will succeed Moses as army commander as well as law mediator.

Moses makes the same request for peaceful passage in 2:26-29 that he earlier made in Seir and Moab, but here because of the Lord's intent, the request provokes war. In 2:30, the phrase, "The Lord your God hardened his spirit and made his heart obstinate," recalls the Lord's earlier dealings with Pharaoh in Exodus. Sometimes the Lord (Exod 4:21; 7:3-5), sometimes Pharaoh (Exod 8:15, 32; 9:34) hardens his (Pharaoh's) heart. Here as elsewhere, the Bible upholds both human freedom and divine sovereignty without exploring the problem of the relation of the two. In short, Sihon freely resists, yet the Lord is somehow over it all. Israel has to fight, yet "the Lord our God gave him over to us" (2:34). To "utterly destroy," so *RSV,* "to place under the ban," or "to devote" is shocking to moderns. The practice of annihilation of enemies reflects the belief that all the spoils of war, people and property, belong to the victorious divine warrior who alone is responsible for victory. The booty is given over to the deity by consecrating it, i.e., by placing it in the divine realm. Material goods, gold and silver, are easily removed from the profane sphere and placed in the diety's temple. But human beings are removed from the profane world and placed in the other world by being killed. It is not known how widely "utter destruction" was practiced in Israel but the usage is so deeply woven into the early traditions it must have played a substantial role in the early days. Israel believed that the Lord alone assigned territory to each nation and that no deity and no king could stand in the way of that exercise of royal power. The rebels of Israel had declared that the walls of the cities were too high (1:28). The present believing generation finds no wall too high, for the Lord goes before them (2:36).

The impression is given in Moses' request to the king for passage that Transjordan was not originally part of the land promised to the ancestors but has been granted now because of the obstinacy of Sihon, " . . . only let me pass through on foot . . . until I go over the Jordan into the land which the Lord our God gives to us'' (2:28-29).

Og of Bashan in 3:1-7 is dealt with in a manner similar to Sihon, except that here no embassy of peace is recorded. Verses 8-10 state concisely that the whole of the Transjordan region north of Moab now belongs to Israel. Og's bedstead (v. 11) was apparently still on display in the Deuteronomist's day. The very sight of it would make the beholder appreciative of the mighty power of the Lord in conquering Bashan.

MOSES DISTRIBUTES THE TRANSJORDANIAN LAND TO THE TWO AND A HALF TRIBES
3:12-22

> [12]"When we took possession of this land at that time, I gave to the Reubenites and the Gadites the territory beginning at Aroer,which is on the edge of the valley of the Arnon, and half the hill country of Gilead with its cities; [13]the rest of Gilead, and all Bashan, the kingdom of Og, that is, all the region of Argob, I gave to the half-tribe of Manasseh. (The whole of that Bashan is called the land of Rephaim.
>
> [18]"And I commanded you at that time, saying, 'The Lord your God has given you this land to possess; all your men of valor shall pass over armed before your brethren the people of Israel.
>
> [21]"And I commanded Joshua at that time, 'Your eyes have seen all that the Lord your God has done to these two kings; so will the Lord do to all the kingdoms into which you are going over. [22]You shall not fear them; for it is the Lord your God who fights for you.' ''

Moses recalls to his hearers that the battles on the Transjordanian side of the land are over. Sihon and Og defied the Lord and were defeated in holy war; their lands are now Israel's. Moses, the leader of the people in war and in peace, distributes the territory, a task fully as sacral as leading holy war. The sequence of holy war, followed by distribution of conquered land, will be repeated when Israel crosses the Jordan and takes the land under Joshua. Indeed the sequence provides the very structure· of the Book of Joshua. Joshua 1-12 are concerned with the military campaigns and chaps. 13-21, with the distribution of the land to the tribes. The modern reader's unfamiliarity with the ancient place names and boundaries in the allotment lists has led to widespread neglect of the lists. But to ancient people, familiar with the contours of their own land, these accounts would be a precious legitimation of the divine origin of their tribe's and family's claims. The allotment is part of the celebration of the completion of holy war. To the divine warrior, the one truly responsible for victory, belong the spoils—prisoners, weapons and equipment, and the land. The war over, Moses then allots the Transjordanian land to the tribes of Reuben, the oldest son born of Leah, to Gad born of Zilpah, and to the half-tribe of Manasseh. Joseph had two sons, Manasseh and Ephraim, and in some reckonings of the twelve tribes the House of Joseph is called by the names of his two sons. Verses 14-15 detail the allocation of the territory to the half-tribe of Manasseh. Machir is a clan of Manasseh. Note the personalizing of the activity. Instead of a simple listing of borders, the actions of the founder, Jair, are described. For the Reubenites and the Gadites in vv. 16-17, the natural boundaries consist either of wadis, i.e., seasonal rivers, or of rivers like the Jabbok in the north, the Arnon in the south, and the Jordan on the west from Chinnereth (Sea of Galilee) to the Salt (Dead) Sea. Verses 12-17 are somewhat obscure. Verses 12-13 proceed from north to south and vv. 14-16 from south to north.

In vv. 18-20 Moses tells "you," i.e., the two and a half tribes, that they cannot settle down in their territory but must march with their as-yet-landless fellow Israelites until all have been given land. At the end of the entire campaign, Joshua will say, "And now the Lord your God has given rest to your brethren, as he promised them; therefore turn and go to your home in the land where your posses-sion lies, which Moses the servant of the Lord gave you on the other side of the Jordan'' (Josh 22:4). Israel is one peo-ple and must act in concert if they are to possess the land.

Moses gives a command at the same time to Joshua (vv. 21-22), another instance in this speech of the handing on of the Mosaic task. Joshua is to let his eye-witness experience of the Lord's defeat of the two kings be a pledge of the defeat of the great kingdoms across the Jordan. He is to adopt the stance of the faithful warrior—unlimited trust in the warrior God who fights for him in the heavenly world. The victories over the two kings and the allotment of the land are a sign, a small sample of the great things to come. The same divine power that is at work today in the small will be at work tomorrow in the great.

JOSHUA TAKES ON MOSES' ROLE
3:23-28; 31:1-8; JOSH 1:1-11

> [23]"And I besought the Lord at that time, saying, [24]"O Lord God, thou hast only begun to show thy servant thy greatness and thy mighty hand; for what god is there in heaven or on earth who can do such works and mighty acts as thine? [25]Let me go over, I pray, and see the good land beyond the Jordan, that goodly hill country, and Lebanon.' [26]But the Lord was angry with me on your account, and would not hearken to me; and the Lord said to me, 'Let it suffice you; speak no more to me of this matter. [27]Go up to the top of Pisgah, and lift up your eyes westward and northward and southward and eastward, and behold it with your eyes, for you shall not go over this Jordan. [28]But charge Joshua, and en-courage and strengthen him; for he shall go over at the head of this people, and he shall put them in possession of the land which you shall see.' "
>
> **31** So Moses continued to speak these words to all Israel. [2]And he said to them, "I am a hundred and twen-ty years old this day; I am no longer able to go out and

come in. The Lord has said to me, 'You shall not go over this Jordan.' ³The Lord your God himself will go over before you; he will destroy these nations before you, so that you shall dispossess them; and Joshua will go over at your head, as the Lord has spoken. ⁴And the Lord will do to them as he did to Sihon and Og, the kings of the Amorites, and to their land, when he destroyed them. ⁵And the Lord will give them over to you, and you shall do to them according to all the commandment which I have commanded you. ⁶Be strong and of good courage, do not fear or be in dread of them: for it is the Lord your God who goes with you; he will not fail you or forsake you.''

⁷Then Moses summoned Joshua, and said to him in the sight of all Israel, ''Be strong and of good courage; for you shall go with this people into the land which the Lord has sworn to their fathers to give them; and you shall put them in possession of it. ⁸It is the Lord who goes before you; he will be with you, he will not fail you or forsake you; do not fear or be dismayed.''

1 After the death of Moses the servant of the Lord, the Lord said to Joshua the son of Nun, Moses' minister, ²''Moses my servant is dead; now therefore arise, go over this Jordan, you and all this people, into the land which I am giving to them, to the people of Israel. ³Every place that the sole of your foot will tread upon I have given to you, as I promised to Moses. ⁴From the wilderness and this Lebanon as far as the great river, the river Euphrates, all the land of the Hittites to the Great Sea toward the going down of the sun shall be your territory. ⁵No man shall be able to stand before you all the days of your life; as I was with Moses, so I will be with you; I will not fail you or forsake you. ⁶Be strong and of good courage; for you shall cause this people to inherit the land which I swore to their fathers to give them. ⁷Only be strong and very courageous, being careful to do according to all the law which Moses my servant commanded you; turn not from it to the right hand or to the left, that you may have good success wherever you

go. ⁸This book of the law shall not depart out of your
mouth, but you shall meditate on it day and night, that
you may be careful to do according to all that is written
in it; for then you shall make your way prosperous, and
then you shall have good success. ⁹Have I not commanded you? Be strong and of good courage; be not
frightened, neither be dismayed; for the Lord your God
is with you wherever you go."

¹⁰Then Joshua commanded the officers of the people,
¹¹"Pass through the camp, and command the people,
'Prepare your provisions; for within three days you are
to pass over this Jordan, to go in to take possession of
the land which the Lord your God gives you to
possess.' "

The excerpts from this section of the speech show that
31:1-8 continues directly upon 3:28. Verse 29 was inserted
to situate chap. 4 at a later date. Deut 4:3 mentions the
apostasy to Baal Peor and so v. 29 places the whole speech
of chap. 4 at Beth Peor. Josh 1:1-10 is added not because it
is a part of the Deuteronomic speech but simply to show
the reader how the entire speech of chaps. 1-3 and 31:1-8 is
introductory to the Deuteronomistic History. The subsequent history of the people in the land is rooted in the word
given through Moses.

Moses had informed his hearers back in 2:14-16 that all
"the evil generation" of the Kadesh-barnea rebellion had
died out, the signal for the Lord to return to Israel's side in
power. Each success since that time has raised the troub-
ling question—what about Moses? Is he a member of the
generation excluded by divine oath (1:34-35, 37)? Verses
23-28 record a delicate dialogue between the servant (a
friend and administrative associate, not a slave) and the
Lord, a dialogue at once personal and official. At the same
time as he prepares Joshua for his role, Moses prays that
he himself see the culmination of divine glory in the land as
he had seen its beginnings in Transjordan. To paraphrase
the prayer: "O Lord, you have shown your servant only

the first of the deeds which demonstrate your glory, that is, your complete control of events in heaven and earth. No power anywhere in the universe is a match for you. Let me see, I pray, the completion of your works which show that you alone are the Lord, the only God.'' Moses is not simply asking to remain in office until his task is done. He is asking to see more of the Lord in his mighty works and in his land. People of that time did not believe in an afterlife where one saw God in the heavens. Moses here really seeks the Lord in his earthly manifestations. He is refused his heart's desire because of the people's sin (v. 26) and is told never to bring up the subject again. He may go to the top of Mt. Pisgah and look from afar on the land he cannot have. A look must suffice for Moses' personal needs. Then he must be about his administrative task to commission Joshua as his successor.

Deuteronomy 31:1 is resumptive of the passage ending in 3:28, and is most naturally translated and interpreted, ''Moses went [from the place where he was praying] and spoke these words [not the words following, but what he had just been told by the Lord about Joshua] to all Israel [i.e., publicly].'' The shift in persons from first to third in the verse is not a difficulty in Hebrew rhetorical style and may indeed be due to a redactor. In public, Moses mentions as reason for his resignation only his feeble condition, not the oath of exclusion: ''I am a hundred years old.'' ''To go out'' and ''to come in'' is a merism, i.e., the mention of a pair standing for a whole series of acts in between. Moses is no longer able to go about freely.

In the sight of all the people, Joshua is now commissioned as leader. As Moses was the speaker of the law given at Horeb, as he was the leader in holy war and in the distribution of the captured land, so Joshua will be for Israel in the future. The great deeds of the Lord do not end with the death of Moses; they will continue because Mosaic leadership is transferable. Where ''Moses'' lives in his designated successors, there Israel has access to the law and to the deeds of the Lord.

Josh 1:1-11 makes use of Deuteronomic language to portray Joshua as the new Moses. It is the genius of the Bible to portray the great servants of the Lord not only with all their endearing human traits and weaknesses but also with public roles greater than their private virtues. When these servants die, they continue to serve, for their office endures.

Section 2.
The Consequences
of False and True Worship
4:1-40

THE LORD WILL GIVE THE LAND TO OBEDIENT ISRAEL EVEN IN EXILE.
4:1-40

(A)   **4** "And now, O Israel, give heed to the statutes and the ordinances which I teach you, and do them; that you may live, and go in and take possession of the land which the Lord, the God of your fathers, gives you.

(B)   ²You shall not add to the word which I command you, nor take from it; that you may keep the commandments of the Lord your God which I command you.

(C)   ³Your eyes have seen what the Lord did at Baal-peor; for the Lord your God destroyed from among you all the men who followed the Baal of Peor; ⁴but you who held fast to the Lord your God are all alive this day.

(A)   ⁵Behold, I have taught you statutes and ordinances, as the Lord my God commanded me, that you should do them in the land which you are entering to take possession of it. ⁶Keep them and do them; for that will be your wisdom and your understanding in the sight of the peoples, who, when they hear all these statues, will say, 'Surely this nation is a wise and understanding people.' ⁷For what great nation is there that has a god so near to it as the Lord our God is to us, whenever we call upon him? [8]And what great nation is there, that has statutes and ordinances so righteous as all this law which I set before you this day?

(B)   [9]"Only take heed, and keep your soul diligently, lest you forget the things which your eyes have seen, and lest they depart from your heart all the days of your life; make them known to your children and your children's children—

(C)   [10]how on the day that you stood before the Lord your God at Horeb, the Lord said to me, 'Gather the people to me, that I may let them hear my words, so that they may learn to fear me all the days that they live upon the earth, and that they may teach their children so.' [11]And you came near and stood at the foot of the mountain, while the mountain burned with fire to the heart of heaven, wrapped in darkness, cloud, and gloom. [12]Then the Lord spoke to you out of the midst of the fire; you heard the sound of words, but saw no form; there was only a voice. [13]And he declared to you his covenant, which he commanded you to perform, that is, the ten commandments; and he wrote them upon two tables of stone.

This speech of Moses resembles chaps. 1-3 + 31:1-8, the "outer frame," in its use of Israel's traditions to make its homiletic point, but it differs from the first speech, and indeed from the speeches of chaps. 5-11, in its perspective. It was written during the Exile of 587-539 B.C. to a nation pondering from afar their Lord and their land. To understand the exilic perspective of chap. 4 and also of chaps. 29-30, one must recall what has been said earlier about the formation of Deuteronomy. Into chaps. 1-3 + 31:1-8, the original introduction of the Deuteronomistic History, the great mass of old material in chaps. 5-28 was inserted. At either end of this material, Mosaic speeches relevant to the Exile were added. Chapter 4 is the first addition, chaps. 29-30, the second. How can a speech of the sixth century be put on the lips of Moses? asks the modern reader. The answer is hinted at in the first speech, just examined, in which the leadership role of Moses *vis-à-vis* the law and the land is handed on to Joshua. In chap. 5 the permanence of the Mosaic office is restated and in 18:15-22 as well: "The Lord your God will raise up for you a prophet like me from among you, from your brethren—him you shall heed (18:15)." In all of these speeches Israel is in its perennial position of looking to its Lord in crisis and Moses is ever there to address them regarding the land on which they are to live.

Whether vv. 1-40 form a coherent address is a controverted question among scholars. A single train of thought is not at first apparent and there is alternate use of second person singular and plural, "thou" and "you." Norbert Lohfink has pointed out that the alternation of singular and plural had probably become a deliberate feature of Deuteronomic style suited to exhortation. The train of thought is clear enough if one follows the leads within the text and refrains from Western modes of analysis.

The speech has drawn upon the covenant formulary for some of its ideas and its structure. The covenant formulary was the outline of a covenant-making ceremony that persisted in the West-Semitic world from the mid-second millennium up to and beyond the time of Deuteronomy. Minor details, e.g., the injunction not to change the wording of the document (v. 2), as well as important features, e.g. the blessings and curses (vv. 21-31), the ample use of historical review (vv. 3, 10-13, 19b-20), the focus on fundamental loyalty or "the Great Commandment" in Lohfink's analysis, all bespeak reliance upon the old formulary. The particular way or structure in which the speech arranges these features is subtle and demands comment before individual verses are commented upon.

Throughout the speech, possession of the land on which Israel is to live is tied closely to obedience to the statutes and commandments given by the Lord through Moses. The connection of obedience to possession of the land, illustrated by the history of the Lord's dealing with the people, is designated "A" in the translation. The second theme, "B," is recognized through reference to the prohibition of images, i.e., the first commandment, and to the Decalogue generally. It always follows the first theme. The third theme, "C," amplifies the preceding through historical example.

A 4:1	A 4:5-8	A 4:14	A 4:21-22
B 4:2	B 4:9	B 4:15-19a	B 4:23-24
C 4:3-4	C 4:10-13	C 4:19b-20	

The repetition of the same scheme provides the redundancy necessary to good oratory. The neat sequence breaks off at v. 24 where, instead of review of the past, there is a prospect on the future: the curses that come upon a disobedient people (vv. 25-28) and the blessings that will follow repentance (vv. 29-31). The peroration (vv. 32-40) is outside the ABC scheme.

Now to the details. The site of the speech is the valley near Beth Peor (3:29, cf., 4:3). In the first ABC sequence (4:1-4), Moses links obedience to the statutes with life in the land. "Life" here is not only physical existence; it means also life in proximity to the Lord, whose very presence means security and *shalom,* "peace." With this nuance, the word "life" and its opposite, "death," often occur in liturgical texts for presence or absence of the Lord. The apostasy at Beth Peor (Num 25:1-12) is the latest instance of Israel's worship of false gods. "All the men who followed the Baal of Peor" in v. 3 is a biblical expression for "give allegiance to" or "worship," the theme of all the other historical reviews of this speech. The chief commandment can be formulated variously, "to fear the Lord," "to love," "to obey the statutes and ordinances," "not to forget Yahweh," but in this speech the first commandment is formulated "to make a graven image," i.e., to bow down to the likeness of a created thing. Those of Israel who spurned Baal of Peor and clung to Yahweh are *alive* today. The way to live then is to cling to Yahweh and reject images of other deities (v. 4).

The second ABC sequence, vv. 5-13, pursues a point similar to the first but with differences in exposition. Moses teaches the statutes in v. 5 that Israel is to learn (see also vv. 1, 10, 14). The emphasis is upon learning rather than hearing, possibly a sign of the shift from liturgical proclamation in the temple to instruction in exilic meetings. How is Israel—without its own land and temple —to present itself to the world, "the nations"? In the temple, the Lord was "near" whenever Israel called upon him (v. 7). The king was the repository of all wisdom, as the Queen of Sheba exclaimed before King Solomon. "The report was true which I heard in my own land of your affairs and of your wisdom, but I did not believe the reports until I came and my own eyes had seen it: and, behold, the half was not told me; your wisdom and prosperity surpass the report which I heard" (1 Kgs 10:6-7). The *torah* in a sense replaces temple and king in the exile. Israel's adherence to it makes them wise and insures the Lord's presence. In v. 9, "B," Israel is "to take heed" and "not forget," expressions used in regard to the great commandment elsewhere in Deuteronomy. Of the traditions of the Lord's appearance at Horeb only the fire on the mountain and the voice speaking the covenantal words engraved upon the two stone tablets are recalled in verses 10-13, "C." The implications from Israel's seeing no form will be drawn later. Here the point is that the *words* of the written covenant reproduce perfectly that primal event of Israel's creation—the Lord speaking out of fire.

The last complete series, vv. 14-20, state even more explicitly than the preceding that the mode of fidelity Israel must show to possess the land is avoidance of idol worship. Israel's particular experience of the Lord at Horeb was in a voice speaking to her and not in any creature of heaven, earth, or underworld (the conventional threefold designation of the universe). The prohibitions quote the first commandment, "you shall not make for yourself a graven image, or any likeness of anything that is in heaven above, or that is in the earth beneath, or that is in the water under the earth; you shall not bow down to them or serve them" (Deut 5:8-9; cf., Exod 20:4-5). Moses adds a prohibition against worship of the heavenly bodies which were thought to present to the earthly worshipper the form of the deities in heaven. "The host of heaven" in verse 19 here means the other deities. In place of *RSV,* read "These (deities) the Lord your God has allotted (Heb. *ḥlq*) to all the peoples under the whole heaven." This view is borrowed (along with other ideas) from the Song of Moses, Deut 32:8, "When the Most High assigned to the nations their territory, / when he differentiated humankind, / he drew the boundaries of the peoples according to the number of the sons of God (*i.e.,* the deities). / But the allotment (Heb. *ḥlq*) of the Lord is his people, / Jacob is his own portion" (slight revision of the *RSV*). In the view of the Song, borrowed here, each nation has its own patron deity which guides its destiny, but Israel belongs to Yahweh, not to one among the deities. Only the Lord has led them from Egypt (v. 20).

The next section, vv. 21-24, concludes not with a historical review of the past, but with a prospect on the future, vv. 25-31. Verses 21-22, "A," connected obedience and possession of land through the example of Moses who suffered exclusion because of the first generation's disobedience (1:37; 3:23-28). Verses 23-24, "B," makes a deft transition from obedience to the covenant amid fire at Horeb to the Lord himself as devouring fire. The mention of the Lord's jealousy, i.e., his passionate refusal to let Israel direct its allegiance to another god, sets the scene for Moses' announcement that a curse will explode upon the people if they disobey (vv. 25-28). One must again recall here the perspective of the speech. It is addressed to exiles who have seen at first hand the curses take effect; they have been driven from the land and scattered among the peoples and have served gods of wood and stone. The last phrase illustrates Israel's view, common in the ancient

East, that the patron god was primarily resident and powerful in his or her own land. To live in a foreign land as an exile was in some sense to be under the patron gods of those lands. In vv. 29-31 the blessing inherent in the covenant takes effect: Israel in exile has the possibility of calling upon its gracious God and of returning to its land.

The peroration, vv. 32-40, sums up the entire speech, with the last verse, v. 40, returning the reader to the first verse, a device called "inclusion." Israel is told to search through the history of other peoples' relation to their gods. Israel's God alone presents himself in awesome fire and in speech, not in the form of any living thing (v. 33). Israel's God alone made his people his own by rescuing them from servitude in Egypt (v. 34). By this Israel recognizes that Yahweh is the only powerful deity, that he alone is God. Verses 36-39 repeat the same injunctions in the same order as vv. 33-35: you have heard the Lord's words, you have seen the Lord's mighty actions in the exodus-conquest. You are to believe in this mighty God. The emphatic mention of the exodus-conquest in vv. 34 and 37-39, especially in the unique description of it as "take a nation for himself from the midst of another nation," is a powerful assurance to a people again captive to foreign gods that they will be brought back into their own land.

In this speech Moses shows himself the instructor of Israel in every age, teaching them how they are to cross over and possess the land even in times of exile.

Section 3. Cities of Refuge in Transjordan
4:41-43

⁴¹Then Moses set apart three cities in the east beyond the Jordan, ⁴²that the manslayer might flee there, who kills his neighbor unintentionally, without being at enmity with him in time past, and that by fleeing to one of these cities he might save his life: ⁴³Bezer in the

wilderness on the tableland for the Reubenites, and Ramoth in Gilead for the Gadites, and Golan in Bashan for the Manassites.

In a short passage duplicated in longer form within the central speech in 19:1-10, Moses sets aside three cities of refuge for perpetrators of unintentional homicide. In a society where a family member was expected immediately to avenge the death of a relative by killing the slayer, often without regard for the motive, cities of refuge functioned as a kind of prison where a trial could be awaited. Why the notice is placed here is not completely clear. It seems closer to 3:12-17 where Moses allots land to the Transjordanian tribes. Assigning cities of refuge in Transjordan at the same time would make sense.

THE SECOND SPEECH.
4:44—28:68

*Section 1. Introduction to the Speech,
Derived from the Covenant Formulary.
4:44-49.*

⁴⁴This is the law which Moses set before the children of Israel; ⁴⁵these are the testimonies, the statutes, and the ordinances, which Moses spoke to the children of Israel when they came out of Egypt, ⁴⁶beyond the Jordan in the valley opposite Beth-peor, in the land of Sihon the king of the Amorites, who lived at Heshbon, whom Moses and the children of Israel defeated when they came out of Egypt. ⁴⁷And they took possession of his land and the land of Og the king of Bashan, the two kings of the Amorites, who lived to the east beyond the Jordan; ⁴⁸from Aroer, which is on the edge of the valley of the Arnon, as far as Mount Sirion (that is, Hermon), ⁴⁹together with all the Arabah on the east side of the Jordan as far as the Sea of the Arabah, under the slopes of Pisgah.

The verses introduce the second (chapters 5-28) of the four speeches of Moses that make up the book. "This law" in v. 44 is defined by v. 45 as "the testimonies, the statutes, and the ordinances," a reference to the detailed legislation that follows. The three words defining "this law" mean respectively "obligation" (arising from a covenant oath, traditionally translated "testimony"), "prescriptions," and "legal decisions." The very site of the assembly, defined carefully in vv. 46-49, adds significantly to the meaning of the speech that follows. It is Beth-peor where Israel committed the great apostasy described in Numbers 25. It is a reminder that the people can all too easily choose another god in preference to Yahweh, a major theme in the following sermons. More positively, Beth-peor is a place in the land that Yahweh has just won for Israel (Deut 2:24—3:17), and hence a reminder of the gracious God who confronts them in the sermons.

Section 2. Sermons on the Great Commandment Derived from the Historical Prologue of the Covenant Formulary 5:1—11:32

MOSES, MEDIATOR OF THE DECALOGUE. 5:1—6:3

5 And Moses summoned all Israel, and said to them, "Hear, O Israel, the statutes and the ordinances which I speak in your hearing this day, and you shall learn them and be careful to do them. ²The Lord our God made a covenant with us in Horeb. ³Not with our fathers did the Lord make this covenant, but with us, who are all of us here alive this day. ⁴The Lord spoke with you face to face at the mountain, out of the midst of the fire, ⁵while I stood between the Lord and you at that time, to declare to you the word of the Lord; for you were afraid because of the fire, and you did not go up into the mountain. He said:

⁶" 'I am the Lord your God, who brought you out of the land of Egypt, out of the house of bondage.

⁷" 'You shall have no other gods before me.

⁸" 'You shall not make for yourself a graven image, or any likeness of anything that is in heaven above, or that is on the earth beneath, or that is in the water under the earth; ⁹you shall not bow down to them or serve them; for I the Lord your God am a jealous God, visiting the iniquity of the fathers upon the children to the third and fourth generation of those who hate me, ¹⁰but showing steadfast love to thousands of those who love me and keep my commandments.

¹¹" 'You shall not take the name of the Lord your God in vain: for the Lord will not hold him guiltless who takes his name in vain.

¹²" 'Observe the sabbath day, to keep it holy, as the Lord your God commanded you. ¹³Six days you shall labor, and do all your work; ¹⁴but the seventh day is a sabbath to the Lord your God; in it you shall not do any work, you, or your son, or your daughter, or your manservant, or your maidservant, or your ox, or your ass, or any of your cattle, or the sojourner who is within your gates, that your manservant and your maidservant may rest as well as you. ¹⁵You shall remember that you were a servant in the land of Egypt, and the Lord your God brought you out thence with a mighty hand and an outstretched arm; therefore the Lord your God commanded you to keep the sabbath day.

¹⁶" 'Honor your father and your mother, as the Lord your God commanded you; that your days may be prolonged, and that it may go well with you, in the land which the Lord your God gives you.

¹⁷" 'You shall not kill.

¹⁸" 'Neither shall you commit adultery.

¹⁹" 'Neither shall you steal.

²⁰" 'Neither shall you bear false witness against your neighbor.

²¹" 'Neither shall you covet your neighbor's wife;

and you shall not desire your neighbor's house, his field, or his manservant, or his maidservant, his ox, or his ass, or anything that is your neighbor's.'

²²"These words the Lord spoke to all your assembly at the mountain out of the midst of the fire, the cloud, and the thick darkness, with a loud voice; and he added no more. And he wrote them upon two tables of stone, and gave them to me."

Chapters 5-11 adapt elements of the venerable covenant formulary, particularly the historical prologue which detailed the past relations of the suzerain and the vassal, in order to lay a basis for a future relationship of loyalty and mutual support. The historical prologue is formed into speeches: 5:1—6:3; 6:4-25; 7; 8; 9:1—10:11 and 10:12—11:17. The first of these Mosaic addresses, 5:1—6:3, is prefatory to the others, detailing the fullness of the covenant demands and legitimating Moses as the covenant speaker.

Moses begins his sermon, "Hear, O Israel, the statutes and the ordinances which I speak in your hearing today" (v. 1), an authoritative summons founded in the people's realization that when Moses speaks they relive the Horeb encounter. The perspective of verses 2-5 differs from that of the speech of chaps. 1-3 + 31, "the outer frame." Unlike that speech, in which the original generation was wiped out in the forty-year wilderness period, prior to entry (see esp. 1:34-35 and 2:14-16), it is here assumed that Moses' immediate hearers were also present at Horeb. The "fathers" in v. 3 are not the first generation distinct from the present group but, as elsewhere in these speeches, the patriarchs to whom the land was given in a promissory rather than a conditional covenant, 7:8, 12; 8:18.

The patriarchal covenant, or promise, had indeed granted the land to the patriarchs and their descendants (see among other places, Gen 12:1-3; 17:8) and that promise is still in force. The Horeb covenant moves from olden promise to lively encounter in which Israel's actual possession of the land is made dependent on their fidelity to the statutes and ordinances of Yahweh.

Having reminded his hearers of the distinctive mutuality of their pact with God, he goes on to recall his part in the original covenant. Moses' underscoring of his mediational role ("While I stood between the Lord and you at that time") in v. 5 and also in 5:22b, 27-28, 31 and 6:1 is not egocentric musing. Rather it makes plain that Israel cannot experience the mutuality of covenant-making unless Moses stands between them and the Lord.

The commandments themselves, vv. 6-21, are virtually the same as in Exod 20:1-17, with the addition that the sabbath rest is for slaves as well as owners since Israel once was a slave in Egypt. The commandments have been numbered differently in Christian tradition. Anglicans, Greek Orthodox, and the Reformed tradition reckon the prohibitions relating to false worship as two, whereas Roman Catholics and Lutherans, following St. Augustine, count them as one and make up the number ten by splitting up the last commandment forbidding covetousness into two.

The first commandment is really vv. 6-10, verse 6 being the grounds for Yahweh's lordship over Israel—he rescued them from servitude to Pharoah to become his servants—and vv. 7-8 prohibiting the expression of servitude to any God but Yahweh. In the ancient East the patron god or gods of a nation and royal house "presented" themselves to their votaries by means of a statue or image. The image, resembling by its form the deity itself in the heavenly world, "becomes" the deity for the worshipper. The likeness need not be elaborate. The resemblance can be stylized and impressionistic. Such likenesses were the ordinary ancient Eastern way of encountering deity. Israel is not to reach Yahweh through images, since none "presents" him. Any image-worship by Israel would mean rejection of the lordship of Yahweh established in Egypt by his victory over Pharaoh. It would provoke Yahweh's jealousy, i.e., his passionate desire that Israel in its totality, i.e., "to the third and fourth generation," be loyal to him alone.

Already in vv. 7 and 8, one meets two formulations of the first commandment. As the subsequent Mosaic speeches will show, the first commandment is not simply the first in a series of ten. It is the fundamental commandment which can be specified further by a variety of statutes. Loyalty to Yahweh alone among the many possible fundamental allegiances that an Eastern people could have—this is the first and greatest commandment. The great commandment is expressed in a variety of phrases in the speeches—to love, to fear, i e., revere the Lord, to keep the commandments, not to forget the Lord. And the specific manner in which Israel is to be loyal to its Lord was also pluriform, e.g., the Ten Commandments, but also lists of different specifications in Exod 34:10-28; Psalm 15, and Ezekiel 18.

Taking the name in vain means swearing false oaths especially in court. To honor the parents ratifies the family network in which the Israelite lived. "Kill" in v. 17 refers to unlawful homicide, not to the taking of all life. Stealing in all probability refers to kidnapping, stealing of other kinds being prohibited by the final commandment regarding the neighbor's household. The word "covet" in v. 21, as new comparative evidence now suggests, means not a mental attitude alone but the initiation of action to seize property. Deuteronomy differs from Exod 20:17 in *not* including the wife as part of the man's chattel.

Such was the extent of "the ten words" inscribed by the Lord on two stone tablets and entrusted to Moses (v. 22). There follows in vv. 23-33 a solemn decision made by the legitimate representatives of the people, the heads of the tribes and the elders, to appoint Moses as official covenant officer. Their motive is religious awe before the majesty of the Lord. Experience had shown that few survived the sudden wrenching from the profane world entailed by intensive encounter with the All Holy. They had survived once. They might not be so lucky again and so they ask Moses to "stand between." The Lord approves that reverence toward the divine word. Moses then stands before the Lord to hear the Lord's words in order to teach them to Israel.

Verses 32-33, framed with the you-plural rather than the you-singular expected in speech between the Lord and Moses, is probably to be taken as a sample of the sermons Moses will later preach to the people after being instructed by the Lord. "The way" or path on which Israel is to walk is a long-lived idiom, preserved even in the New Testament for "a way of life." The *RSV* should be corrected: "You shall turn neither right nor left on the whole path which the Lord your God has commanded you to walk so that you may live, etc."

It is official! Moses is the mediator with the full agreement of the people and the approval of the Lord. There follows now a summary, really a sample of what will follow in chaps. 6-11. "This is the commandment" in 6:1 is introductory, stating that Moses will teach what he has been told to teach (5:31). A sample of his future themes is 6:2 which states in two different formulations the great command—to fear the Lord, to keep his statutes and commandments. The last verse, "Hear, O Israel," 6:3, repeats the first verse in 5:1, leading the Semitic hearer to recall the opening sentence and to realize that the speech has come full circle to its close.

Moses has established in his sermon that it is the people's desire and the Lord's will that he officiate when the Lord presents himself in his covenantal words. Only so is there authentic encounter. Through Moses' office Israel has the opportunity again and again to enter that dialogue with the Lord in which they recognize his unique claims and hear his "jealousy" for them. In this speech one finds the office of covenant mediator of which Joshua is the most famous example after Moses (see the outer frame). Within this concern the passage from the Great Code makes sense. "The Lord your God will raise up for you a prophet like me from among you, from your brethren— him you shall heed—just as you desired of the Lord your

God at Horeb on the day of assembly, when you said, 'Let me not hear again the voice of the Lord my God, or see this great fire any more, lest I die.' And the Lord said to me, 'They have rightly said all that they have spoken. I will raise up for them a prophet like you from among their brethren; and I will put my words in his mouth, and he shall speak to them all that I command him. And whoever will not give heed to my words which he shall speak in my name, I myself will require it of him" (Deut 18:15-19).

ISRAEL IS TO LOVE THE LORD ALONE
UPON ENTERING THE LAND
6:4-25

⁴"Hear, O Israel: The Lord our God is one Lord; ⁵and you shall love the Lord your God with all your heart, and with all your soul, and with all your might. ⁶And these words which I command you this day shall be upon your heart.

¹⁰"And when the Lord your God brings you into the land which he swore to your fathers, to Abraham, to Isaac, and to Jacob, to give you, with great and goodly cities, which you did not build, ¹¹ and houses full of all good things, which you did not fill, and cisterns hewn out, which you did not hew, and vineyards and olive trees, which you did not plant, and when you eat and are full, ¹²then take heed lest you forget the Lord, who brought you out of the land of Egypt, out of the house of bondage. ¹³You shall fear the Lord your God; you shall serve him, and swear by his name. ¹⁴You shall not go after other gods, of the gods of the peoples who are round about you;

²⁰"When your son asks you in time to come, 'What is the meaning of the testimonies and the statutes and the ordinances which the Lord our God has commanded you?' ²¹then you shall say to your son, 'We were Pharaoh's slaves in Egypt; and the Lord brought us out

of Egypt with a mighty hand; ²²and the Lord showed signs and wonders, great and grievous, against Egypt and against Pharaoh and all his household, before our eyes; ²³and he brought us out from there, that he might bring us in and give us the land which he swore to give to our fathers. ²⁴And the Lord commanded us to do all these statutes, to fear the Lord our God, for our good always, that he might preserve us alive, as at this day. ²⁵And it will be righteousness for us, if we are careful to do all this commandment before the Lord our God, as he has commanded us.' ''

The sermon of 6:4-25 assumes that Moses has been selected by the people and ratified by the Lord as liturgical mediator whose homiletic words Israel is to embrace in order to become the Lord's people (chap. 5). As in the other sermons of chaps. 5-11, the topic is the chief commandment of the covenant but specified by the particular situation of Israel—here the danger of abandoning Yahweh in Israel's discovery of the already cultivated land.

The chapter uses for its frame a type of old ritual text like that of Exod 13:11-16 (cf., also Exod 12:25-27 and 13:5-10). The old texts link rites of a later time with the primal events of the exodus-conquest. When the rite is celebrated, the original event is experienced anew by the later generation. The framework consists of a parallel statement with slight variation, "When the Lord brings you into the land . . . you shall do [a ritual act] . . . // When in time to come your child asks you, 'What does this [rite] mean?' you shall say to him, 'By strength of hand the Lord brought us out of Egypt . . . ' '' The texts make use of the familiar device of parallelism to show that the Lord took care during the very occurrence of the great deeds of old that later generations would be able to participate in that power.

Our text changes and deepens the old ritual texts. Instead of commanding the performance of a rite through which Israel of a later age can encounter the God of the exodus-conquest, Deuteronomy 6 proposes "these words" (v. 6) and "these statutes" (v. 24) through which Israel is able to be fundamentally loyal to its God, to love and to revere him, to observe the commandments.

Within the traditional report of the institution of the rite, the elements of the speech take on their particular meaning. Verses 4-9 preface the parallel structure of vv. 10-19 and 20-25. Within this preface, vv. 4-5 are the divine demand and vv. 6-9 outline the response. The translation of v. 4 is controverted. The context of the entire speech urges a revision of *RSV* to "Hear O Israel, Yahweh is our God, Yahweh alone." Israel is about to enter a land already cultivated by another people (vv. 10-11) with the help of their agricultural deities. Like any near Eastern people, Israel is liable to worship these gods whose patronage by the peoples had led to their prosperity. So the injunction is given at the threshold of the new land that Israel is not to divide its religious attention among several gods, goddesses, and Yahweh. Since there is only one deity, Yahweh, all of Israel's attention and energy (whole heart, etc.) is to be directed to him. The fact that love is commanded here is not surprising if one remembers that love in the context is not love in the Western romantic tradition, but deeply affectionate loyalty directed toward a person worthy of that love. Verses 6-9 make the love of v. 5 equivalent to carrying out the commandments of the Lord, an equivalence found also at the end of the speech in vv. 24-25. "These words" are to enter deeply into people and spread through their whole life and environment (vv. 6-9) so that the full dimensions of the love may be always comprehended. Jews of a later age correctly sensed that the essence of their religion lies buried in v. 5 and recited it twice daily. The confession of faith is called the *Shema* from its opening word, "Hear." They also turned the metaphor of v. 8 into a literal command, inscribing Exod 13:1-10, 11-16 and Deut 6:4-9; 11:13-21 on tiny pieces of parchment. They were placed in tiny boxes and bound on the forehead and left arm, the "phylacteries" of the NT period, at the time when the *Shema* was recited. Jesus, in the Gospel of Matthew, 22:34-40, of Mark, 12:28-34, and of Luke, 10:25-28, refers his questioners to the same text which summed up for him, as it did for Moses' hearers, the first and greatest response of Israel to God's offer.

The full meaning of the first parallel, vv. 10-15, becomes clear only when read with the second member of the parallelism, vv. 20-25. Varying slightly the form of the old texts in Exodus, the sermon envisions Israel discovering a land already wondrously settled and civilized by other peoples ("goodly cities which you did not build," etc., vv. 10-11). The Israelite, like every other ancient near Easterner, would be tempted to ascribe the prosperity of the land to the heavenly power of its patron god(s) and hence render worship to them. It is precisely at this moment that Moses proposes the most appropriate formulation of the great commandment—do not forget Yahweh whose power was first seen not in the prosperity of this land but in the rescue from Egypt. Verses 13-14 are various formulations of the command. Even "to swear by his name" is to revere only the Lord since the true worshipper of Yahweh will invoke only Yahweh and no other in an oath. In v. 15, as in 5:9, Yahweh is jealous when his own people violate the first commandment and go after other gods.

Verses 16-19 is an appendix to the first half, showing by a reference to the incident at Massah (Exod 17:1-7) that Israel has already in the wilderness period "forgotten" their God and that it should be all the more wary not to forget and to test the Lord again in the land. In the Bible to "test" means to put someone in a situation where that person's true mettle or orientation becomes clear. God may test us but we may never test God.

The second part, vv. 20-25, clarifies and completes the first part. In the old texts of cultic institution, the child asked for the meaning of a ritual, e.g., the rite of sprinkling blood on the door posts. Here the child asks for the meaning of "the testimonies and the statutes and or-

dinances." Performing these statutes is like performing the
ritual—it puts the performer in touch somehow with the
old exodus-conquest (vv. 21-23). Performance of the
statutes means "life" and "righteousness" which have a
special liturgical meaning here—nearness to the Lord.
Those who observe the statutes are near the Lord.

Moses warns Israel, about to enter the land, to love
Yahweh alone, and not to divide its loyalty among the
"gods" who allegedly made the land prosperous. Israel is
to encounter its Lord and his redemption in keeping "these
words" and "these statutes." By fidelity to the Lord
preached in the word, Israel will indeed come to love its
Lord.

ISRAEL IS TO REMAIN FAITHFUL TO
THE LORD IN THE FACE OF TEMPTATIONS FROM
THE SEVEN NATIONS.
CHAP. 7

7 "When the Lord your God brings you into the land
which you are entering to take possession of it, and
clears away many nations before you, the Hittites, the
Girgashites, the Amorites, the Canaanites, the Periz-
zites, the Hivites, and the Jebusites, seven nations
greater and mightier than yourselves, ²and when the
Lord your God gives them over to you, and you defeat
them; then you must utterly destroy them; you shall
make no covenant with them, and show no mercy to
them.

⁷It was not because you were more in number than
any other people that the Lord set his love upon you and
chose you, for you were the fewest of all peoples; ⁸but it
is because the Lord loves you, and is keeping the oath
which he swore to your fathers, that the Lord has
brought you out with a mighty hand, and redeemed you
from the house of bondage, from the hand of Pharaoh
king of Egypt. . . . ¹⁶And you shall destroy all the
peoples that the Lord your God will give over to you,

your eye shall not pity them; neither shall you serve their gods, for that would be a snare to you.

[17]"If you say in your heart, 'These nations are greater than I; how can I dispossess them?' [18]you shall not be afraid of them, but you shall remember what the Lord your God did to Pharaoh and to all Egypt,

[22]The Lord your God will clear away these nations before you little by little; you may not make an end of them at once, lest the wild beasts grow too numerous for you. [23]But the Lord your God will give them over to you, and throw them into great confusion, until they are destroyed."

That chap. 7 is a single sermon with a consistent point of view is not so obvious as in the speech of 6:4-25 where the adaptation of the old two-part ritual text strongly suggests one original hand, or in chap. 8 where a single formal structure dominates. The theme, the annihilating of the original inhabitants, is abhorrent to modern readers. The task of analysis has been of little interest. No clear formal structure emerges, but only an outline based upon content. Nonetheless, the speech deals in a unified way with a perennial issue for Israel, its behavior as a holy or separate people amid the surrounding peoples and its stance toward them—whether and why Israel should accommodate or separate. Moses' final answer will be, not unexpectedly, that Israel will find its identity by total obedience to the Lord, being careful to do all his statutes. But the reasoning and the illustrations that lead to that conclusion are portrayed in an imaginative way.

A brief outline will suggest some of the unity and flow of ideas.

7:1-6. After the Lord gives Israel the land, they must "devote" or extirpate the seven great nations lest they persuade Israel to worship their gods. Otherwise the anger of the Lord would break out and destroy Israel. Israel, among all the peoples of the earth, is the special possession of Yahweh.

7:7-11. Yahweh has passed over those great nations in order to set his love upon Israel whom he has chosen freely by taking them from Pharoah's control. Yahweh is their God, "reliable" in that he is faithful to those who revere him and hostile to those who hate him. Keep his commandments to remain in his favor (v. 11).

7:12-15. If Israel obeys, the blessings reserved for Yahweh's friends will be theirs in abundance, and recognizable particularly in the fertility of the land. The curses will fall on their enemies (v. 15).

7:16-21. Israel must destroy the peoples who persist in occupying the land which now belongs to Israel as lovers of Yahweh and keepers of his covenant (compare vv. 9 and 12). Though the nations are bigger than they are, Israelites are to believe that Yahweh will bring against the mighty nations the military power unleashed once against Egypt. As there was no need to fear defeat in Egypt, there is no need to fear now.

7:22-26. In reverting to the vocabulary and sentence structure of vv. 1-2, suggested by italic type below, the last section subtly qualifies the original command. "The Lord your God *will clear away the nations before you. . . . the Lord your God will give them over to you. . . .* he will give their kings into your hand . . . you shall make their name perish from under heaven" (vv. 22-24). Here the Lord clears away the nations little by little, not all at once. The peoples will continue to surround them after their taking of the land, making all the more necessary hostility toward them, lest they seduce Israel into worshipping their deities.

There is a single theme in chap. 7, though different stages of editing are visible. Israel is not to let its small size among the surrounding nations awe or frighten it into making treaties and alliances with them. Israel's Lord is the master of the nations. He has given the land they occupy to Israel. The conquest is to be seen as divine protection for Israel's uniqueness among the nations.

The details of the chapter fit this interpretation. The number of the nations Israel will face in their war of conquest is seven, a biblical number often suggesting completeness. These historical enemies represent all those nations that persuade Israel to join them and abandon its status as Yahweh's peculiar possession. The seven peoples, though mentioned elsewhere in the Bible, cannot all be identified with certainty. The Jebusites lived around Jerusalem and the Hittites may have been an Anatolian colony in Palestine. Amorite is the usual Deuteronomic designation for the pre-Israelite inhabitants—Canaanites in other traditions. The important point is the representative number seven and the greater might and size of the nations. Israel will always be smaller and weaker than its neighbors and will be tempted to worship their neighbors' gods, who presumably have bestowed those very blessings of might and size upon them.

Israel's smallness and seeming insignificance are important features in the sermon (vv. 1, 7, and 17). How can so small a nation be the people of the Lord? The answer is that the size or strength of a people means nothing to Yahweh (v. 7) who chooses freely out of fidelity to his promise to the patriarchs (v. 8) and takes a people for himself out of the hands of the most powerful ruler, the king of Egypt (v. 8). When the seven nations are displaced from their territory, Israel must annihilate them. The same language has been seen in the sermon of chapters 1-3 + 31, the outer frame, in regard to Sihon king of Heshbon and Og king of Bashan. Yahweh is the sole victor to whom the rules of war assign all booty, human and material. Human beings are to be transferred out of the profane into the sacred world of Yahweh by being killed. No treaties, e.g., making the nations into subject peoples or obligating them to pay tribute, are to be made (v. 2). Treaties were always made under the patronage of the gods of the parties involved; hence they would involve Israel with a god other than Yahweh. The prohibition comes not from a sense of superiority but from a sense of danger to Israel. The other nations will persuade Israel to worship their gods alongside of Yahweh. Yahweh's anger would break out as it must in the case of the people's infidelity, and Israel would lose its one basis of identity in a world of large powers, that it is the Lord's people (v. 6). Verse 6 makes sense only within the polytheistic world of the ancient East. Israel is holy, dedicated, not to any of the "gods," but to Yahweh. Israel is "his own possession," (Heb. *segulla),* a word occurring also in the famous passage of Exod 19:4-6, and meaning a possession of the god or king.

The second section, vv. 7-11, emphasizes that the loving and totally free choice of Yahweh is unrelated to Israel's size or accomplishments. Blessings and curses are in store for his friends and enemies. What determines the value and prestige of a nation therefore is not its size or power but the Lord's attitude toward it. This secret of national greatness, consoling to Israel, at the same time divests Israel of all reason to boast—or to fear.

In the third section, vv. 12-15, v. 12 draws out v. 11: Israel's observance of the Great Commandment, here formulated as hearkening to the ordinances—is to be Israel's entry into the true greatness bestowed by the Lord. The abundance of life that comes with the Lord's favor will be theirs and the evil that comes upon his enemies will come upon Israel's enemies. Israel's distinctiveness among the nations will not be its size but the blessings of the covenant. "You shall be blessed above all peoples." The blessing is chiefly abundance of life in the land.

In vv. 16-21, Israel is exhorted to carry on the holy war. To enter into battle with reckless courage, laying aside fear and trusting in the divine warrior who achieves victory—this is the attitude Israel is to have when they cross the Jordan. The might of the nations may tempt Israel to give up the fight to possess the land. But the Lord who chose them as his possession by taking them from the control of a powerful nation, Egypt (vv. 7-8), will complete that same act of choosing by giving them the land. The "hornets" of v. 20 is a traditional translation of an unknown Hebrew word: it could be the panic that was considered a weapon of the gods in sacral wars of antiquity.

The last section, vv. 22-26, generalizes the military advice for a campaign into a strategy to be used by all generations of Israelites who seek to possess the land on which they are to live. The nations will not be cleared out instantly. They will be there to "ensnare" (v. 25) Israel always. Ultimately they will be destroyed by the hand of the Lord, but meantime Israel is to maintain its exclusive allegiance to the Lord, carefully excluding from their homes those objects of worship which would mean violation of the first commandment.

ISRAEL IS TO LIVE BY DIVINE COMMANDMENT IN THE LAND AS IT LIVED BY MANNA IN THE WILDERNESS
CHAP. 8

> **8** "All the commandment which I command you this day you shall be careful to do, that you may live and multiply, and go in and possess the land which the Lord swore to give to your fathers.
>
> ¹¹"Take heed lest you forget the Lord your God, by not keeping his commandments and his ordinances and his statutes, which I command you this day: . . . ¹⁸You shall remember the Lord your God, for it is he who gives you power to get wealth; that he may confirm his covenant which he swore to your fathers, as at this day. ¹⁹And if you forget the Lord your God and go after other gods and serve them and worship them, I solemnly warn you this day that you shall surely perish. ²⁰Like the nations that the Lord makes to perish before you, so shall you perish, because you would not obey the voice of the Lord your God."

The previous Mosaic addresses within chaps. 5-11 have amply demonstrated how Israel unerringly focussed on the great commandment yet interpreted it with sensitivity according to its different situations. In chap. 8 Moses envisions how Israel must hear the Lord's word after it is settled in the land and prospering. "Take heed lest . . . when you have eaten and are full, and have built goodly houses and live in them, and when your herds and flocks multiply, and your silver and gold is multiplied, and all that you have is multiplied, then your heart be lifted up . . . then . . . you forget the Lord your God. . ." (vv. 8-14). The phrase, "to forget the Lord your God" is here, as in 6:12, a statement of fundamental apostasy, an act Israel is in danger of committing at any stage in its history.

How will Moses persuade the people to fundamental loyalty to the Lord when they prosper in the land? How will he bring vividly before their eyes the dangers that lurk in the very blessings of the covenant? Moses' method of persuasion is the posing of a dramatic contrast between two historical periods: the desert period when Israel was led and fed miraculously in a hostile dry environment (vv. 2-6 and 14-17) and the settlement period when Israel experiences fertile land and prosperous culture (vv. 7-10 and 12-13). Dramatic contrast is inherent in Hebrew rhetoric. Bible readers are familiar with it in "Hebrew parallelism," a balance in form and thought between successive lines in a poem. The contrasts can be larger than verses; they can be located in extended figures of speech, e.g., Dame Wisdom and Dame Folly, Yahweh and Pharaoh, or in rival themes as here. The Semitic audience evidently had a developed capacity to attend to several depictions at once and could intuit the resonances. This speech develops the contrasts between desert and land, the unsown and the sown, through a concentric structure, also called chiasm (from the Greek letter "X" or chi). The analysis by Norbert Lohfink is followed here.

8:1	A			Fundamental command
8:2-6		B		Desert
8:7-10			C	Cultivated land
8:11			A	Fundamental command
8:12-13			C	Cultivated land
8:14-17		B		Desert
8:18-20	A			Fundamental command

The word "today" (*RSV* "this day") occurs in all three commands, vv. 1, 11, 18-20 (2x), reminding us that these sermons were for delivery to a liturgical assembly who would confront in the Mosaic preacher's words the Lord's exodus-conquest and respond accordingly. Life in the land hangs upon Israel's fundamental obedience, their not deviating from the commandments. The first portrayal of the desert (vv. 2-6) emphasizes divine pedagogy. In Hebrew education or "discipline," one learned by the experience of the inherent consequences of a good or bad course of action. The Lord "humbles," i.e., makes one aware of one's dependence, and "tests," i.e., puts one in a position where one's true orientation appears. The old traditions about the wilderness are rearranged with great liberty. There is nothing here of the familiar topic of infidelity in the wilderness. New details are added, e.g., the miraculous protection of foot and clothing in v. 4. The desert is the schoolroom where Yahweh controls the environment. He cuts off the supply of ordinary food so that the manna might appear clearly for what it actually is—miraculous food making Israel realize it lives from what comes from the mouth of God. The Hebrew word for "what proceeds from" the mouth of God, *môṣā'*, resembles the word for commandment in v. 1, *miṣwah*. In the desert Israel lived off manna coming from the mouth of God; in the land it will live from the commandment coming from the mouth of God. Verse 6 transposes the desert "way" of v. 2, the route through the desert, to the metaphorical "way" or pattern of life.

To the rhetorically heightened depiction of the desert in vv. 2-6 is juxtaposed the similarly heightened depiction of the land, flowing with water, lush with fruit, filled with metallic ore. The contrast is not between the sterility of the desert and the fertility of the land. It is rather between the direct and visible nurturing of God in the wilderness and the indirect and invisible nurturing in the land. The power is divine in both spheres but it requires a different kind of sight to sense the divine power in the land. The Lord to be sure gives the land, but then the land delivers its own goodness without the dramatic visibility of divine nurture in the desert.

When the people, satisfied with the land's natural abundance, bless the divine giver of the good land, they must take care not to forget their Lord who taught them in the desert not to live only from bread (v. 3) but also from the divine word demanding absolute fidelity. The danger is further specified in the second picture of the cultivated land, vv. 12-13. The nuance here is the culture that Israel constructs in the fertile land. The vigorous massing of personal resources to construct the human city can easily lead to deep forgetfulness of the Lord who is behind all strength and glory. Again the desert period is portrayed as a place of testing, of fierce contrasts between a hostile environment and a protecting God (vv. 14-17). The stunning evidence of divine protection made it impossible for Israel to credit itself with its own salvation. Only in the land could that thought arise (v. 17).

The third and climactic command (vv. 18-20), warns Israel not to forget their youthful education, that period when the Lord disciplined them to experience unmistakably his presence. Direct and miraculous intervention of the Lord belong to the olden days. Israel is called to recognize in the "natural" fertility of the land and in their own energetic cultivation of it that everything, the land's fertility and their own power, are Yahweh's gifts. Not to recognize the Lord is dangerous. It puts Israel in danger of being expelled like the nations who also did not recognize the Lord's hand in the wonders of the land.

NOT ISRAEL'S RIGHTEOUSNESS BUT THE LORD'S GRACE GIVES THE LAND
9:1—10:11

> **9** "Hear, O Israel; you are to pass over the Jordan this day, to go in to dispossess nations greater and mightier than yourselves, cities great and fortified up to heaven,

²a people great and tall, the sons of the Anakim, whom you know, and of whom you have heard it said, 'Who can stand before the sons of Anak?' ³Know therefore this day that he who goes over before you as a devouring fire is the Lord your God; he will destroy them and subdue them before you; so you shall drive them out, and make them perish quickly, as the Lord has promised you.

⁴"Do not say in your heart, after the Lord your God has thrust them out before you, 'It is because of my righteousness that the Lord has brought me in to possess this land'; whereas it is because of the wickedness of these nations that the Lord is driving them out before you. ⁵Not because of your righteousness or the uprightness of your heart are you going in to possess their land; but because of the wickedness of these nations the Lord your God is driving them out from before you, and that he may confirm the word which the Lord swore to your fathers, to Abraham, to Isaac, and to Jacob.

⁶"Know therefore, that the Lord your God is not giving you this good land to possess because of your righteousness; for you are a stubborn people. ⁷Remember and do not forget how you provoked the Lord your God to wrath in the wilderness; from the day you came out of the land of Egypt, until you came to this place, you have been rebellious against the Lord. ⁸Even at Horeb you provoked the Lord to wrath, and the Lord was so angry with you that he was ready to destroy you.

²⁵"So I lay prostrate before the Lord for these forty days and forty nights, because the Lord had said he would destroy you. ²⁶And I prayed to the Lord, 'O Lord God, destroy not thy people and thy heritage, whom thou hast redeemed through thy greatness, whom thou hast brought out of Egypt with a mighty hand. ²⁷Remember thy servants, Abraham, Isaac, and Jacob; do not regard the stubbornness of this people, or their wickedness, or their sin, ²⁸lest the land from which thou

didst bring us say, "Because the Lord was not able to bring them into the land which he promised them, and because he hated them, he has brought them out to slay them in the wilderness." ²⁹For they are thy people and thy heritage, whom thou didst bring out by thy great power and by thy outstretched arm.'

10 "At that time the Lord said to me, 'Hew two tables of stone like the first, and come up to me on the mountain, and make an ark of wood. ²And I will write on the tables the words that were on the first tables which you broke, and you shall put them in the ark.' ³So I made an ark of acacia wood, and hewed two tables of stone like the first, and went up the mountain with the two tables in my hand. ⁴And he wrote on the tables, as at the first writing, the ten commandments which the Lord had spoken to you on the mountain out of the midst of the fire on the day of the assembly; and the Lord gave them to me. ⁵Then I turned and came down from the mountain, and put the tables in the ark which I had made; and there they are, as the Lord commanded me.

¹¹And the Lord said to me, 'Arise, go on your journey at the head of the people, that they may go in and possess the land, which I swore to their fathers to give them.' "

Even in the few verses excerpted above, the repetitions of thought are plainly visible. These suggest successive editings of biblical traditions. The statement in v. 4, that it is not because of Israel's righteousness but because of the nations' wickedness that Yahweh is bringing Israel in to possess the land, is repeated in vv. 5 and 6., The sequence of events in 9:18-29 is not clear: Moses' prostration is twice reported (vv. 18 and 25). Verses 22-24 seem to introduce matter extraneous to the rest of the speech. More evidence of later commentary expanding an original shorter speech could be adduced. This commentary will concentrate on the text as finally shaped, a text which, for all its complex history, makes a coherent statement.

Like the other Mosaic speeches, this one is addressed to

Israel in a particular moment in their life on the land—the moment when the people proudly declare that their own righteousness placed them in possession of the land. "Righteousness" in this context usually means proximity to the Lord and the resultant divine favor and protection. For Israel to speak of "my righteousness" means that it is claiming ownership and disposal over the Lord's free gift. Such an assault on grace illustrates a profound forgetting of the Lord which violates the Great Commandment.

It is also a forgetting of their own history. Moses must then review their appalling record of infidelity even at the point of their origin, Horeb. "Remember and do not forget how you provoked the Lord your God to wrath in the wilderness. . . . Even at Horeb. . . " (9:7-8). Moses' review of the sin at Horeb is largely a reworking of the traditions in Exodus 32-34, which give an account of the apostasy of the people in worshipping the golden calf, their punishment for this offense, the renewal of the covenant and Yahweh's promise to go with the people by means of his angel, his presence and his name. All these elements have been recast in Deut 9:1-10:11 with the same artistry that Deuteronomy 7 used in recasting the traditions in Exod 23:20-33.

Moses, entrusted with the two stone tablets, here seen not so much as the Ten Commandments but rather as the record of the dealings of Yahweh with the people, is sent down by Yahweh to see the people violating the first commandment—making a molten image of a living thing. Moses breaks the tablets—nullifying the previous agreements between God and the people. His prayers to avert total destruction of the people are successful and a new set of tablets is made showing divine forgiveness. In the traditions of Exod 34:1-4, the Deuteronomist makes a highly significant change: he introduces the ark, the wooden container for the tablets. In fact, the ark is mentioned four times in five verses (Deut 10:1-5), seemingly with more emphasis than the tablets! The Levites also are introduced, as bearers of the ark and mediators to the peo-

ple of the divine blessings it contains. Moses is told by the
Lord to go in at the head of the people (10:11). The climactic command sums up the main concern of Exodus 34, to
show how the Lord will continue to go among the sinful
people to lead them to Canaan.

Moses then said to the Lord, "See, thou sayest to me,
'Bring up this people'; but thou hast not let me know
whom thou wilt send with me. . . ." And he said, "My
presence will go with you, and I will give you rest [*i.e.,*
grant you the land]. And he [Moses] said, "If now I have
found favor in thy sight, O Lord, let the Lord, I pray thee,
go in the midst of us, although it is a stiff-necked people
. . . ." (Exod 33:12,14; 34:9)

The people have apostasized and only at Moses' prayers
has the Lord forgiven them. The people are nowhere
depicted as repenting. As in Exodus 32-34, the question is:
does the apostasy mean the Lord will not lead them in the
land? The answer here is a resounding no! Yahweh will go
in front, not in his presence or in his angel according to
the old Exodus traditions, but in his words on the tablets in
the Ark of the Covenant, carried by the tribe of Levi.
Moses thus has effectively countered the temptation of
Israel to credit themselves and their righteousness for the
victory.

A detailed examination supports the general interpretation given above. Verses 1-6 are largely concerned with the
theme of divine leadership in the wilderness and conquest,
a theme which figures very prominently in the Sinai traditions in Exodus 23 and 32-34. In the traditions of Exodus
and Deuteronomy the giving of the law on the holy mountain is part of the journey to possess the Promised Land. A
major question in these traditions which generally emphasize God's holiness and transcendence and Israel's sin-
fulness is how the all-holy God can dwell with the sinful
people. These texts avoid saying simply that Yahweh will
go before, but use surrogates for the divine presence,
"Behold I send an angel before you, to guard you on the
way and to bring you to the place which I have prepared.

Give heed to him and hearken to his voice; do not rebel against him, for he will not pardon your transgressions; for my name is in him (Exod 23:20-21; cf. v. 23)." The great apostasy raises anew the question of divine guidance. "If for a single moment I should go up among you, I would consume you" (Exod 33:5). The presence of the Lord in his "face" or "presence" (Exod 33:14-16) and in his angel (Exod 32:34 and 33:2) after their great sin has been forgiven is a totally undeserved gift of God, granted in place of the annihilation they deserve. It is then truly blasphemous for Israel to claim that her virtue caused their God to clear away the nations. Three reasons are given in the text itself against the claim: firstly, the nations are being expelled for their wickedness by the Lord of the universe who alone "allots" heritages, i.e., assigns territory to each people. Secondly, Yahweh is fulfilling his word of promise to the ancestors to give land to their descendents; and thirdly, Israel in the divine judgment is "stiff of neck" (*RSV* "stubborn").

The last point, v. 6, Israel as stiff necked, is illustrated within the rest of the speech. Israel is rebellious at its origin. Moses' fast of forty days and nights forms a frame around the account of the people's sin, vv. 99 and 18. It emphasizes the separation from the profane world of eating and drinking when dealing with God in heaven. Throughout the entire episode Moses is shown as separate from the sinful people, close to the awesome transcendent Lord.

Moses the covenant mediator breaks the stone tablets (v. 17) containing the words which the Lord had spoken in fire with the people on the day of assembly (v. 10). Israel's worship of the molten calf (v. 16) violates the first commandment against images of any sort (5:8-9). As Moses realizes, the people are in danger since an outbreak of divine jealousy can be expected for violation of the command against images. "For I was afraid of the anger and hot displeasure which the Lord bore against you so that he was ready to destroy you" (v. 19). Moses laments for the whole people. Even the priest Aaron is not exempt from the danger. The sin at Horeb will be repeated in rebellions in other sites (vv. 22-24). Moses is shown prostrate and lamenting before the Lord (v. 18) and in vv. 25-29 the content of his prayer is revealed. In biblical laments, the petitioner seeks to persuade God to act for him, often with considerable oratorical skill. The three motives that Moses uses to persuade God are similar to the three used to convict Israel in the first part of the speech, vv. 4-6. Do not regard the hardness of the people and their sin (v. 27b). Call to mind your promise of land to the patriarchs and to their seed and your earlier commitment in Egypt (vv. 26-27a, 29), and let not the wicked judgments of the nation, Egypt, prevail (v. 28).

That Moses' prayer is answered is shown by God's direct response, that he hew two new tablets of stone to be engraved by the divine hand (10:1). Moses is instructed also to fashion a wooden container for the tablets, the ark, so that they can be carried. As stated earlier, the Deuteronomist has introduced the ark here which is absent in the Exodus version. In Exodus the ark is described in 25:10-21;31:1-11; 35:30—36:1; 37:1-9. The ark is evidently seen here as the container of the tablets which will be borne by the Levites in the march to the land. Moses does not hesitate to link Aaron the priest to the apostasy (9:20). Asserting the important role of the Levites in carrying the ark of the covenant and conveying to the people the power of that presence (by blessing in the name, 10:8-9) would be a dramatic statement of renewal of covenant and of the presence of the Lord with his people. A typically Deuteronomic characterization of the mode of presence is expressed in the old traditions: the Lord now goes before the people in the tablets of stone in the ark, on which the finger of God wrote "all the words which the Lord had spoken with you on the mountain out of the midst of the fire on the day of the assembly" (9:10). In these Deuteronomic speeches, "devouring fire" is the source of the words and it is reasonable to associate the "devouring fire'' that destroys the nations and subdues the land in 9:3 with the words contained in the ark. The reinstatement of the covenant is complete in 10:11 with the command to Moses to journey at the head of the people to lead them into the land.

To the people's temptation to credit their own nobility for the successful taking of the land, Moses opposes their apostasy at Horeb when they came within a hair's breadth of annihilation. They are to realize that their continuance in existence as Yahweh's people is owed to the Lord's fidelity to his own word.

THE ONE LORD WHO RULES HISTORY IS THE LORD WHO RULES THE FERTILITY OF THE LAND
10:12—11:17

[12]"And now, Israel, what does the LORD your God require of you, but to fear the LORD your God, to walk in all his ways, to love him, to serve the LORD your God with all your heart and with all your soul, [13]and to keep the commandments and statutes of the LORD, which I command you this day for your good? [14]Behold, to the LORD your God belong heaven and the heaven of heavens, the earth with all that is in it; [15]yet the LORD set his heart in love upon your fathers and chose their descendants after them, you above all peoples, as at this day. . . . [21]He is your praise; he is your God, who has done for you these great and terrible things which your eyes have seen. [22]Your fathers went down to Egypt seventy persons; and now the LORD your God has made you as the stars of heaven for multitude.

11 [2]And consider this day (since I am not speaking to your children who have not known or seen it), consider the discipline of the LORD your God, his greatness, his mighty hand and his outstretched arm, [3]his signs and his deeds which he did in Egypt to Pharaoh the king of Egypt and to all his land; [4]and what he did to the army

of Egypt, to their horses and to their chariots; how he
made the water of the Red Sea overflow them as they
pursued after you, and how the LORD has destroyed
them to this day; ⁵and what he did to you in the
wilderness, until you came to this place; ⁶and what he
did to Dathan and Abiram the sons of Eliab, son of
Reuben; how the earth opened its mouth and swallowed
them up, with their households, their tents, and every
living thing that followed them, in the midst of all
Israel; ⁷for your eyes have seen all the great work of the
LORD which he did.

¹⁰For the land which you are entering to take possession of it is not like the land of Egypt, from which you
have come, where you sowed your seed and watered it
with your feet, like a garden of vegetables; ¹¹but the
land which you are going over to possess is a land of
hills and valleys, which drinks water by the rain from
heaven, ¹²a land which the LORD your God cares for; the
eyes of the LORD your God are always upon it, from the
beginning of the year to the end of the year.

From the opening, "And now, Israel, what does the
Lord your God require of you . . .," the sermon breathes
the air of liturgical proclamation to an Israel in the temple
court assembled to respond to their Lord. Here one finds
the artful blending of Israel's response in love (the Great
Commandment) and Yahweh's deeds that initiate the relationship, along with the blessing and the curse hidden in
that relationship. The old covenant formulary with its
history of the relation between suzerain and vassal, and its
blessings and curses provides once again a powerful model
for a sermon to the Lord's people.

Only the historical recitals are printed above in order to
illustrate with what emphases and details the national story
of exodus-conquest is narrated. (Deuteronomy usually includes as well the promise to the patriarchs.) Interspersed
between the history are the various formulations of the
Great Commandment: to fear the Lord, to love him, to
walk in his ways, to serve (i.e., worship) him with all one's

spirit, to cling to him, to swear by his name, to keep his commands (always in that order). At the end, vv. 13–17, the blessings and curses are mentioned, though the parallel between obedience and blessings in v. 15 and disobedience and curses has been obscured by the change of v. 16 from a conditional to a hortatory sentence.

The outline:

10:12–13		The Great Commandment
14–15	(16)	Yahweh chooses the patriarchs (and appended exhortation)
17–18	(19)	Yahweh king of heaven and earth
20		The Great Commandment
21–22		Yahweh multiplies the people in Egypt
11:1		The Great Commandment
2–7		Yahweh masters the waters, the wilderness, and the earth
8–9		The Great Commandment
10–12		Yahweh makes the land fruitful
13–17		Blessings and curses inherent in the land

One concern dominates. How will Israel recognize their Lord in their new agricultural world? Up to this moment God has revealed himself in the historical events of the exodus-conquest. Moses demonstrates to them that Yahweh is a God of cosmic power, ruling the entire universe in the historical events of the exodus-conquest.

Each part of the speech is related to the other in a brilliant synthesis. The commandments are not simply stark demands to be obeyed by an Israel grateful for past acts of God. The Lord rather initiates the freed human response through his activity. Hence in the speech one finds commandment embedded in historical recital.

The total commitment expressed in the piling up of five different formulations of the Great Commandment, vv. 12–13, is immediately grounded in the Lord's choosing of

the patriarchs, vv. 14–15. The background of the language
is polytheism; each nation or group had its patron deity,
one among many in a vast pantheon. But Israel has as its
patron not one of these minor deities but the only powerful
God, Yahweh, who has chosen "your fathers," the
patriarchs. He has also in the same act chosen "their seed"
(*RSV* "their descendants"), you of this generation. Even
in the patriarchal period, Yahweh's word was connected
with human fertility and procreation. As "we" of this
generation were somehow there in the patriarchs, the command to circumcise given to them can be adapted to us:
circumcise the foreskin of your hearts, a metaphor undoubtedly influenced by its parallel, literally "no longer
stiffen your necks." The heart was considered, not the seat
of feelings, but of intelligence. The patriarchal generation
is, in the Deuteronomic view, a time of promising the land
to Abraham, Isaac, and Jacob (6:10), entered into by circumcision (10:16). But only the present generation has
heard the specific divine demands of the Horeb covenant.
Hence the old rite of circumcision practiced by patriarch
and present generation alike must have an added depth of
meaning for the Horeb generation.

In vv. 17–18, a reference to the national story would be
expected since the speech elsewhere alternates command
and story. Instead one finds a depiction of Yahweh the
king of the heavens or the divine world ("the God of gods
and Lord of lords") and earth, where his rule is described
through verbs of activity rather than by adjectives. Ancient
Eastern kings emphasized their sponsorship of a legal
system which defended the poor, "the widow and the or-
phan," and the sojourner, the foreign resident whose
rights would be easy to slight. Israel's behavior toward
foreign residents is linked to the divine attitude in v. 19,
analogous to v. 16 in its brevity and concreteness. A three-
member series of commands follows in v. 20 upon the announcement of kingship.

A second element of the sacred story is noted in vv.

21-22, the increase of the people in Egypt, from seventy persons to the number of the stars in the heavens. Yahweh's ability to enhance his people's fertility in order to fulfill his promise to make them like the stars for multitude (Deut 1:10 and Gen 15:5) is highlighted since Israel will be tempted in the new land to leave behind Yahweh in order to embrace new gods of fertility.

The portrayal of the Lord as the one behind Israel's fertility is the context for the love and obedience demanded in 11:1. "Commandment" is expressed by several synonyms like charge, statutes and ordinances; each has a particular nuance of meaning but when used together, as here, they probably express the totality of God's will. Next in vv. 2-7, this generation of Israel is called upon to remember Yahweh's activity in their history, interpreted not as spectacular activity without qualification, but as "discipline," a lesson intended for the instruction of Israel in the liturgical assembly. His mighty acts show his sovereign control over the waters of the Red Sea, over the sterility of the wilderness, and over the earth (which he commands to swallow Dathan and Abiram). Only a cosmic God could master the divisions of the universe. His control of the land of Canaan will be an easy thing.

The injunction of vv. 8-9 ensures that Israel will indeed possess the land that is vibrant with life from Yahweh's hand. Nothing is said here about Israel's need for military prowess or agricultural skill—only fidelity to the Lord. The characterization of the land as flowing with milk and honey leads to the final segment from the exodus-conquest story: the nature of the land. Instead of the cumbersome artificial water system that irrigates Egypt, Yahweh waters Israel directly from his water supply in the heavens, showing again that God is able to deploy his power in the new situation of Israel.

Israel has heard the word of the Lord from the lives of their ancestors. Now they must choose. Yahweh will be their God, making their land fertile, if they will be his people by serving him alone with all their might (vv. 13–15). The alternative is truly frightening (vv. 16–17). Serving "other gods," the gods Israel might suppose provide the fertility of the land, will lead to death—closed heavens, infertile earth, finally flight from a hostile environment.

Moses puts before Israel a lively portrait of Yahweh who has proved himself not only a God who has saved them from slavery and brought them to the threshold of the land, but also of One who has blessed them continually by giving them life in his universe.

CONCLUSION TO THE FIRST PART OF THE COVENANT FORMULARY (CHAPS. 5–11) AND TRANSITION TO SPECIFIC LAWS OF THE GREAT CODE
11:18–32

[18]"You shall therefore lay up these words of mine in your heart and in your soul; and you shall bind them as a sign upon your hand, and they shall be as frontlets between your eyes. [19]And you shall teach them to your children, talking of them when you are sitting in your house, and when you are walking by the way, and when you lie down, and when you rise. . . . [22]For if you will be careful to do all this commandment which I command you to do, loving the Lord your God, walking in all his ways, and cleaving to him, [23]then the Lord will drive out all these nations before you, and you will dispossess nations greater and mightier than yourselves.

[26]"Behold, I set before you this day a blessing and a curse: [27]the blessing, if you obey the commandments of the Lord your God, which I command you this day, [28]and the curse, if you do not obey the commandments of the Lord your God, but turn aside from the way which I command you this day, to go after other gods which you have not known. [29]And when the Lord your

God brings you into the land which you are entering to take possession of it, you shall set the blessing on Mount Gerizim and the curse on Mount Ebal. [30]Are they not beyond the Jordan, west of the road, toward the going down of the sun, in the land of the Canaanites who live in the Arabah, over against Gilgal, beside the oak of Moreh? [31]For you are to pass over the Jordan to go in to take possession of the land which the LORD your God gives you; and when you possess it and live in it, [32]you shall be careful to do all the statutes and the ordinances which I set before you this day.''

Verses 18-32 appears to be both the conclusion of the series of speeches on the Great Commandment and a pointer, esp. vv. 29-32, to the definitive ceremony of blessing and curse on Mt. Gerizim and Mt. Ebal detailed in chapter 27. They end appropriately with an exhortation to keep the words constantly on one's mind and before one's eyes and to hand them on to the next generation (vv. 18-21). It is a reminder that possession of the Lord's land is not an unconditional grant but is dependent upon one's love of the Lord (vv. 22-25). It places before Israel in a most concrete way the blessings and the curses of the covenant (vv. 26-32). Even though chaps. 5-11 serve as historical prologue to chaps. 12-28, the chapters form a coherent section of their own with their own conclusion in vv. 18-28 and transition (vv. 29-32). As has been seen in the speeches, the influence of the covenant formulary in Deuteronomy extends to far more than simply providing an outline for chaps. 4-28; it also ties the Lord's benefits to Israel, the people's loyalty to the Lord. The recital of divine deeds, the call for response, the emphasis on blessings and curses—all reflect the rhetoric of the formulary.

To conclude these speeches so as to elicit the proper response seems the purpose of 11:18-28. Though almost every verse of vv. 18-25 is an echo of something earlier, e.g., vv. 18-20 of 6:7-9, vv. 21 and 23 of 4:38 and 40, the new configuration makes a new statement. The formulary provided for the recording of the treaty on a tablet and for the periodic recital of its conditions. The vivid metaphors of vv. 18-21, "lay these words of mine in your heart and soul," "bind them as a sign upon your hand . . . as frontlets upon your eyes," no doubt reflect a concern that the original moment of covenant not grow dim with the passing of time and the rise of a new generation. Verses 22-25 is really a blessing, a feature which typically ends the formulary. This blessing is entirely identified with success in conquest of the land, ". . . if you are careful to do all this commandment . . .' then the Lord will drive out those nations before you . . ." Conquest will be entirely the work of God.

In vv. 26-28, the blessings and curses framed in a more traditional way, are vividly portrayed before the people so that they may see the result of their choices. The choice Israel will make on the land will be either for Yahweh as their God or for "other gods." And each choice, each "way," has an inherent energy, a blessing or a curse. The latter part of v. 28 means "to adopt as your gods deities whose protective deeds you have never experienced," in contrast to Yahweh whose mighty acts the Israelites have already experienced in Egypt and in the wilderness journey.

Verses 29-32 ends the first section and introduces the reader to chaps. 12-28, particularly to the ceremony of blessings and curses in chap. 27, where the neighboring mountains of central Palestine, Gerizim and Ebal, are sites of the liturgy. Verse 30 gives directions to the mountains for the first generation who presumably have never been across the Jordan. The first part of Moses' speech is ended. Israel knows that Yahweh is their God and has chosen them from all other peoples. Now they must hear in detail his will so that their response can be comprehensive as well as loving.

Section 3.
Laws Modeled on the Covenant Formulary
12:1—26:19

THE SINGLE SANCTUARY OF THE LORD'S CHOICE
12:1-28

12 "These are the statutes and ordinances which you shall be careful to do in the land which the LORD, the God of your fathers, has given you to possess, all the days that you live upon the earth. ²You shall surely destroy all the places where the nations whom you shall dispossess served their gods, upon the high mountains and upon the hills and under every green tree; ³you shall tear down their altars, and dash in pieces their pillars, and burn their Asherim with fire; you shall hew down the graven images of their gods, and destroy their name out of that place. ⁴You shall not do so to the Lord your God. ⁵But you shall seek the place which the Lord your God will choose out of all your tribes to put his name and make his habitation there; thither you shall go, ⁶and thither you shall bring your burnt offerings and your sacrifices, your tithes and the offering that you present, your votive offerings, your freewill offerings, and the firstlings of your herd and of your flock; ⁷and there you shall eat before the Lord your God, and you shall rejoice, you and your households, in all that you undertake, in which the Lord your God has blessed you.

¹⁵"However, you may slaughter and eat flesh within any of your towns, as much as you desire, according to the blessing of the Lord your God which he has given you; the unclean and the clean may eat of it, as of the gazelle and as of the hart. ¹⁶Only you shall not eat the blood, you shall pour it out upon the earth like water. ¹⁷You may not eat within your towns the tithe of your

grain or of your wine or of your oil, or the firstlings of
your herd or of your flock, or any of your votive offerings which you vow, or your freewill offerings, or the
offering that you present; [18]but you shall eat them
before the Lord your God in the place which the Lord
your God will choose, you and your son and your
daughter, your manservant and your maidservant, and
the Levite who is within your towns; and you shall rejoice before the Lord your God in all that you undertake. [19]Take heed that you do not forsake the Levite as
long as you live in your land."

Verse 1, "these are the statutes and ordinances," echoes
similar announcements earlier in the book, 1:1; 4:1;
4:44–45; 5:1; the reference here is to the specific laws of
chaps. 12–28. The sermons of chaps. 5–11 are introduced
by the same terms, showing that the book does not
distinguish as sharply as many moderns do between fundamental option and specific act. The act instances the attitude and the attitude expresses itself in concrete actions.
Verses 2–28 is concerned with the single sanctuary
which Yahweh will choose (vv. 4–14) and the allowance of
non-sacral slaughter of animals, a change of practice dic-
tated by the requirements of a single sanctuary (vv. 15–27).
The demand to destroy all non-Yahwistic shrines in vv. 2–3
prefaces laws about the single Yahwistic shrine in vv. 4–28.
First, there is to be only one sanctuary, chosen by the Lord
(vv. 4–7), repeated with slight variation in vv. 8-12, to
which is appended a summational conclusion in vv. 13–14.
Second, non-sacral killing and eating of animals is permitted outside of the single shrine in vv. 15–19, repeated with
slight variation in vv. 20–27, to which is appended an ex-
hortatory conclusion in v. 28.
The so-called centralization of worship law has puzzled
commentators. From the time of David (ca. 1000–961
B.C.), who centralized the old religious traditions in his
city of Jerusalem, "the place which the Lord your God will

choose out of all your tribes to put his name" would certainly be understood as Jerusalem. Moses, of course, would not name Jerusalem in this speech since several hundred years would have to elapse before David made Jerusalem the central shrine. He likewise does not name the cities of refuge in the land in 19:1-3. But it seems to have been the general practice prior to the formation of Deuteronomy in the late eighth century to allow a multiplicity of altars: in Mosaic law from very early times (Exod 20:24) and in practice through much of the monarchic period (1 Kgs 3:2, 3; 2 Kgs 16:4 among many passages). In addition, Lev 17:1-9, which in its present form legislates that all slaughtered animals were to be brought to the Tent of Meeting, probably in its original form stated that the animal was to be brought to any one of numerous altars throughout the land. For how could every animal slain be carried fifty or sixty miles to a *single* shrine? Exod 20:24, an old text, shows that many altars were permitted in the ancient law. "An altar of earth you shall make for me and sacrifice on it your burnt offerings and your peace offerings, your sheep and your oxen; *in every place* where I cause my name to be remembered I will come to you and bless you." In addition, one learns from the books of Joshua, Judges, and Samuel that Israel upon entrance into the land went to a succession of central shrines, Gilgal, Shechem, Shiloh. Thus there were in Israel traditions both of a central shrine and also of a multitude of altars.

The difficulty posed by Moses' insistence here upon a single shrine from the very beginning in the light of contrary law and practice is eased considerably if one keeps in mind the Deuteronomic perspective. The shrine "represents" the deity to the people. One encounters one's god in the place selected by the god. The multiplicity of gods that the pre-Israelite inhabitants worshipped is reflected in the very large number of holy places, in natural phenomena such as hills and luxuriant trees and in artifacts such as upraised slabs or "pillars," "asherim" (trees or wooden poles), and statues. The one Lord, on the contrary, is "re-presented" in one shrine. The land is now Yahweh's and his people's. Consequently true worship means wiping out any vestige of the so-called gods of the displaced inhabitants, their "names," and positively it means regular attendance at the place or shrine the Lord chooses.

There is another obvious reason for a single shrine, hinted at in v. 9, "for you have not as yet come to the allotted rest (*RSV* "the rest and the inheritance") which the Lord your God gives you." Ancient Hebrew poetry spoke of Yahweh leading Israel through the wilderness to his own dwelling where his people, safely settled, would celebrate his kingship. Often the divine dwelling was conceived of as a mountain and sometimes the entire land was described as a mountain, the entire space being considered the Lord's holy sphere and dwelling. Exodus 15 is the most famous but by no means the only example of the idea, "Thou hast led in thy steadfast love the people whom thou has redeemed, / / thou has guided them by thy strength to thy holy abode" (v. 13). Cf. also Exod 15:17; Pss 74, 77, 78:42-55 and 67-72. The place which the Lord has chosen is thus the goal of the march of conquest and the dwelling of the victorious Lord. It is appropriately the site where the first fruits of the crops and animals are returned to the Lord who owns the land.

The individual sections elaborate the view that a unique God has swept onto the scene, rendering otiose the many shrines that once represented the old gods, a God who has put his name in only one place. The harsh message of vv. 2–3 to destroy all sanctuaries and equipment forbids Israel simply to take over the worship systems of the dispossessed peoples. A new and unique God must have a new and unique sanctuary, chosen afresh by himself, not inherited from the humiliated deities of the dispossessed. In the verses, "places" means "holy places" and deliberately in its plural form is contrasted with the singular "place" of Yahweh in vv. 5, 11, 13, 14, 18, and 26. Similarly, the "names" of the gods are to be effaced from their shrines so that the "name" of Yahweh can dwell in his shrine.

Israel is not to worship the Lord in an abundance of shrines, located at striking natural locations—so the sense of v. 4. In the East, the deity's presence was discovered in sites that displayed the power of nature, springs, great trees, mountains. Not so in Israel. Their place is holy by divine word of choice. There "the Lord will put his name," an expression rulers had long used in the ancient East to state their rule over a place. One of the Pharaohs in the fifteenth century boasted he had placed his name in Jerusalem. The name represents the person and to put one's name in a place means that people there recognized the authority and presence of the person in that place. The shrine is to be the site of all sacral offerings, the transfer of people's gifts to the divine realm. Burnt offerings and sacrifices are the two commonest forms of sacrifice, the former designating the total burning of an animal upon the altar, the latter, the peace offering in which certain parts of the animal are burned and the rest eaten by the worshipper. The worshipper is linked to God and to fellow Israelites by the shared food. See Lev 1:1-17 and 3:1-17 for further information. Tithes, the annual donation of a tenth of the produce of the soil, is discussed in detail in 14:22-29. "The offering that you present" is an individual's free contribution of money, spoils, or the like. Offerings can be the result of a vow, "votive offerings," or simply spontaneous, "freewill offerings." The firstlings of animals will be discussed under 15:19-23. The rites mentioned are a random sample of all the cultic offerings in which the laity take part and are meant to indicate totality. All sacred rites are to take place within the shrine which the Lord chooses.

The eating and rejoicing of v. 7 refers to the eating of a communal meal in which the food shared effected communion with God and fellow Israelites. The modern reader should keep in mind that the average Israelite visited the temple only a few times a year, and that the visit was a relief from the drab monotony of farm life. A visit was an opportunity not only to attend colorful religious services but also to visit relatives and friends. It was truly a time for rejoicing in the blessings of the Lord (v. 7).

Verses 8-12, a repetition of vv. 4-7 (with vv. 13-14 as the recapitulation), begin with the warning that the elaborate worship system of the wilderness period offers no model for the worship that will take place in the land. Verse 4 had already stated that Canaanite ritual was not to be imitated by the Israelites. The reason is that worship in the wilderness was carried out in a variety of sites, not at the single site chosen by the Lord. People engaged today in periodic reform of the liturgy are wont to forget that in antiquity ritual was not so subject to rational criticism and improvement. One did not chose or design a rite, and still less the place. Rather, the ritual and the right place were pointed out by the deity through a sign. Only on arriving at the goal of the journey, "the allotted rest," could true worship begin. For here was the Lord's land.

As mentioned earlier, vv. 10-12 repeat with variations the commands of vv. 4-9, and in the same sequence. The people are to perform all their sacral acts at the single site chosen by the Lord after they have been given rest from all their enemies by the Lord. The list of those who are to partake of the sacral feast "before the Lord," i.e., in the sanctuary, is expanded to include the Levite. The Levites were assigned no territory of their own (10:9) and so had to depend upon fellow Israelites for their subsistence.

The recapitulation in vv. 13-14 expresses tersely the ancient belief that only God could select the spot for commerce between the heavenly and the earthly world. Only in a shrine may sacred offerings be made.

Verses 15-27 deal with the implications of a single sanctuary. The first section, vv. 15-19, is repeated with slight change in the second, vv. 20-27. If there was to be a single sanctuary for a land that was 150 miles from north to south, how could the old custom remain valid that held all killing of domestic animals—ox, lamb, goat—to be sacral and related at an altar? Lev 17:1-9, to which reference has already been made, stipulates that all such slain animals must be brought to the door of the Tent of Meeting. Originally, in the view of many scholars, the text read "altar of earth." It presumed therefore a great many altars to which it was relatively easy to bring the few animals that would have been slain, outside of game animals. There was not much eating of meat outside of festivals. But with only one altar, a person killing an animal in the city of Dan, for instance, would have had to carry it over 100 miles to Jerusalem! Hence, this revision of the old custom.

An important desacralization takes place in these verses. Not every natural movement or act is automatically sacred, but only those declared so by the Lord. The second part of v. 15 needs to be paraphrased. Any animal, even the ox, lamb, and goat of Lev 17:3, can be killed non-sacrally and reckoned like game, e.g., the gazelle or the deer. Game was not offered in sacrifice. One need not be ritually clean to eat it. Killing and consumption are completely desacralized.

In no case, however, may the blood be consumed, "for the life of every creature is the blood of it" (Lev 17:14). Blood concretized life itself better than any other natural thing. Consuming blood would apparently give to humans mastery over life that only God possesses. Verses 17-18 are the obverse of v. 15. All sacred activity is to take place in the one shrine.

Verses 20-27 repeats vv. 15-19, yet with change. The day will come when the land will simply be too extensive for the old view that regarded all slaughter as sacred and hence needing an altar, "when the Lord your God enlarges your territory . . ." Verse 28 summarizes the whole chapter and promises blessings to those who obey the statutes.

The two-fold repetition in the chapter raises the question whether old traditions have been combined in this chapter. The repetition is most probably not to be taken as evidence of different sources nor, still less, as a sign of successive editions. The chapter is not after all the promulgation of a law pure and simple. It is rather preached law. The divine command to go to only one place, a command which relativizes and desacralizes older custom, is presented to Israel in the most attractive way to gain free assent. Hence the redundancy of oratory, seen before in chaps. 5–11. Moses goes over the material in the same sequence so that the hearer may review more than once the attractiveness and the urgency of the divine command.

SUBVERSION OF THE LORD'S SOVEREIGNTY 12:29—13:18

²⁹"When the LORD your God cuts off before you the nations whom you go in to dispossess, and you dispossess them and dwell in their land, ³⁰take heed that you be not ensnared to follow them, after they have been destroyed before you, and that you do not inquire about their gods, saying, 'How did these nations serve their gods?—that I also may do likewise.' ³¹You shall not do so to the LORD your God; for every abominable thing which the LORD hates they have done for their gods; for they even burn their sons and their daughters in the fire to their gods.

³²"Everything that I command you you shall be careful to do; you shall not add to it or take from it.

13 "If a prophet arises among you, or a dreamer of dreams, and gives you a sign or a wonder, ²and the sign or wonder which he tells you comes to pass, and if he says, 'Let us go after other gods,' which you have not known, 'and let us serve them,' ³you shall not listen to the words of that prophet or to that dreamer of dreams; for the LORD your God is testing you, to know whether you love the LORD your God with all your heart and with all your soul. ⁴You shall walk after the LORD your God and fear him, and keep his commandments and obey his voice, and you shall serve him and cleave to him. ⁵But that prophet or that dreamer of dreams shall be put to death, because he has taught rebellion against the LORD your God, who brought you out of the land of Egypt and redeemed you out of the house of bondage, to make

you leave the way in which the LORD your God commanded you to walk. So you shall purge the evil from
the midst of you.''

Like the preceding chapter regarding the single shrine,
this section is concerned with the Lord's sole sovereignty
over Israel in the land, and in particular with the problem
of those who subvert that sovereignty. In antiquity, people
thought it unwise and even dangerous to neglect the gods
of the land where one resided. In a world intensely sensitive to deities presenting themselves in natural
phenomena, especially deities concerned with fertility, the
Israelite newcomers to Canaan would instinctively set their
Yahweh among the other gods long worshipped in the
land. One would go on to inquire how the nations served,
i.e., worshipped, their gods (12:30) so that one could
follow the customs of each god, "to walk after" the god,
to use the biblical idiom. Polytheism is tolerant and syn-
cretistic. There is always room for one more in the pantheon. Not so with Yahwism. One God means that one's
entire allegiance is entirely directed to One alone, with the
whole heart and soul. Enticements even from the most
authoritative religious voices (13:1–5), from one's closest
and dearest intimates (13:6–11), or from larger groups, to
include other gods alongside of Yahweh, are to be ruthless-
ly purged.

The section is divided into four parts: a prohibition
against learning non-Yahwistic rituals in 12:29–31; v. 32
prefaces the three legal cases which follow: two cases of en-
ticement in 13:1–5 and 6–11, and a case of a locality that
has definitively gone over to other gods in 13:12–18.

The first section, 12:29–31, forbids the adoption of rites
used in the liturgies of the gods of the defeated peoples.
The emphasis upon the dispossession of the peoples is the
most devastating critique of the gods that could be made in
an ancient Near Eastern context. The gods were powerless
to preserve their lands and peoples in the face of Yahweh's
presence. Why then should Israel worship these failures at
divinity?

A second reason for allowing the rites to fall into oblivion is their disgusting nature. The nations sacrificed their own children to their gods! Moses here touches on perhaps the most abhorrent practice of the indiginous inhabitants of the eastern littoral, and of their Phoenician colonies throughout the Mediterranean basin in the first millennium B.C. In Carthage, one of the colonies, a huge number of infant skeletons has been recently excavated, the ages of the children ranging from fetuses to children two or three years old. The sacrifice of the first-born child was done on the same basis as the offering of the first fruits of the land. Fertility was in the hands of the gods. To thank the god for the entire harvest, and to placate the deity so that the land would continue to be fertile, a small amount of produce, "the first fruits," was offered to the god. So with those most precious gifts—children. To thank the god for the fertility of the woman and to ensure future offspring, the first child was given back to the god, transferred to the divine world by death. Israel's Lord might be passionate and might react in fierce anger at sin and injustice. Never did Yahweh make the killing of infants a part of his worship.

Because the three cases that follow contain hard sayings, they are prefaced by 12:32 that no change is to be made in them.

The first case, 13:1–5, counters seductions from the most impeccable religious authorities, the prophets. "The dreamer of dreams" is an honorable title. Dreams were an accepted means of learning the divine will in antiquity. To validate their messages, prophets often provided some kind of token. The token could be a prediction of an event, the fulfillment of which would show the power of the prophet, or some other arresting evidence of access to the gods. But no matter how authenticated by traditional means, the prophet is not to be believed if the message is abandonment of exclusive worship of Yahweh. "Let us go after other gods and let us serve them," is the refrain summing up the propaganda of all seducers, vv. 2, 6, and 13. Everything is subordinate to the first commandment.

Fidelity to Yahweh alone in a polytheistic world is the formulation that all speech must be judged by.

The allurements of the false prophets constitute a testing of Israel, i.e., they place Israel in a situation where its true orientation manifests itself. The false prophet's exhortation to follow other gods forces the people to choose between Yahweh and the others. It will be known whether "you truly love the Lord" (stronger than *RSV*). "Love" in this verse is not mere romantic affect. It is the courageous choosing of the Lord in the face of competing attractions, and the adherence to him with one's whole powers. In the midst of this life and death crisis, the six-fold repetition of formulations of the great commandment in v. 4 is completely understandable. The seducer must be put to death, no matter how great the prestige he or she may enjoy in the community. The mention of the exodus in v. 5 is not by chance. Yahweh created his people by means of that event and they owe to him alone their loyalty. No other "god" is owed anything. The final phrase, "so you shall purge the evil from the midst of you," occurs with slight variations eleven times in Deuteronomy, always at the close of instructions regarding the punishment of a wrongdoer and always, with the exception of 19:19, with a reference to capital punishment. Israel is holy and must purge all sin from itself. In so doing it also offers salutary warnings to would-be evildoers (13:11).

The second case deals with persuasion to worship other gods coming from quite another quarter than public authorities—relatives and friends. The two cases thus exhaust all potential danger sources—public and private. There is danger not only of worshipping the gods of Israel's immediate neighbors but also the gods of far-off peoples. The reference must be to the great empires of antiquity which intruded into Israel's life: Egypt, Assyria, and Babylon. When the latter two nations exercised their hegemony over Israel, they would have brought insignia of their national deities to Jerusalem which would have been publicly displayed as trophies.

The Israelite is not to heed even loved ones. Rather he or she should be the first to denounce and the first to stone to death. Note the realism of v. 8. One is not to let family feelings dissuade one from the denunciation nor is one to shield the guilty one. Such overcoming of natural affection in the service of the Lord could only impress Israel and prevent further rebellion (v. 11).

The third case, vv. 12-18, is that of a locality which has been persuaded to follow after other gods. The danger was always present that whole regions within Israel would include other gods in their loyalties. This case illustrates how belief in Yahweh was the bond uniting Israel into a single people. Their common memory was the story of how he rescued them from bondage to Pharaoh in Egypt and brought them into a land entirely his by reason of conquest of the nations and their gods. They owed nothing to any other god or nation. To pay obeisance to other gods was to be false to that common tradition and risk losing the unity of the tribes. Infidelity of a city or region was not only a denial of Yahweh's rescue which created the people. It also destroyed the basis of their identity as a people.

The punishment for regional apostasy is harsh: annihilation of the city and all its inhabitants. After the investigation, to be done with great care because of the tribal rivalries persistently begetting libelous rumors, the faithless city is to be attacked as if it were a Canaanite city. Holy war is declared and in accord with its principles, the conquered city is placed under the ban. All is to be devoted (*RSV* "utterly destroy") to Yahweh to whom victory belongs. The presence in the midst of Israel of the apostate city constitutes a danger to all, as did the presence of Korah and his companions in Numbers 16 and Achan in Joshua 7.

Three legal cases have been taken from the lawbook and placed on the preacher's podium. Expanded by the meditation of the preacher and theologian, they have now a wider application than they had previously. Even if the Israelite never had occasion to hear blandishments from a false prophet, relative, or renegade region, he or she will have learned from this legal sermon just how serious is the injunction to serve no other God than Yahweh, and how this majestic command rules over every religious, domestic, and civic phenomenon in Israel.

HOLINESS OF THE LAITY
14:1-21

14 "You are the sons of the Lord your God; you shall not cut yourselves or make any baldness on your foreheads for the dead. [2]For you are a people holy to the Lord your God, and the Lord has chosen you to be a people for his own possession, out of all the peoples that are on the face of the earth.

[3]"You shall not eat any abominable thing. [4]These are the animals you may eat: the ox, the sheep, the goat, [5]the hart, the gazelle, the roebuck, the wild goat, the ibex, the antelope, and the mountain-sheep. [6]Every animal that parts the hoof and has the hoof cloven in two, and chews the cud, among the animals, you may eat. [7]Yet of those that chew the cud or have the hoof cloven you shall not eat these: The camel, the hare, and the rock badger, because they chew the cud but do not part the hoof, are unclean for you. [8]And the swine, because it parts the hoof but does not chew the cud, is unclean for you. Their flesh you shall not eat, and their carcasses you shall not touch.

[21]"You shall not eat anything that dies of itself; you may give it to the alien who is within your towns, that he may eat it, or you may sell it to a foreigner; for you are a people holy to the Lord your God.

"You shall not boil a kid in its mother's milk."

The section is at first reading the driest and the least interesting of the entire book. To add uncertainty to aridity, several of the animals and birds are unknown and their

English equivalents are little more than educated guesses. Yet the chapter has interest because of the new context that Deuteronomy had given these ancient laws which are found in another version in Leviticus 11 and because of what they reveal about the holiness of the people. The apt title of the section, "Holiness of the Laity," has been borrowed from the fine commentary of the English scholar, S. R. Driver.

The gist of the section is that Israel is holy to the Lord, i.e., set apart unto the Lord from the profane world in which it lives. The concept of holiness is different from that common in the West today. Holiness in the chapter does not refer primarily to the moral probity of the people but to their being separate and to their belonging to the Lord. To be near to the all holy Lord made one holy. And often it was simply a question of geographical proximity, as if holiness were a physical quality.

One approached holy things or holy places only under strict rules, for there was danger. One was traveling at the margin of one's own world and at the edge of the divine world. It was necessary to have guidance such as rituals and priestly protocol.

Verses 3-21 give a sample of dietary laws observed by the people. It is important to notice the change in intent here from the very similar passage in Lev 11:2-23. Leviticus contains for the most part priestly lore, and in chapters 11-15, laws setting forth the distinction between clean and unclean, i.e., ritually pure and impure. In Lev 10:10 priests are told, "You are to distinguish between the sacred and the profane, and between the unclean and the clean." Deuteronomy has taken priestly lore and made it into preaching, as it had made case law into preaching in chap. 13.

The preface in vv. 1-2 (not in Leviticus 11) provides the context for understanding the specific laws. "Sons" or "children" of the Lord in v. 1 means all those men or women who belong to the Lord. Cutting oneself or shaving the front of the head were mourning rites observed in the worship of other gods. A late second millennium text from the city of Ugarit, a site in what is today Syria, describes similar rites for the dead Baal, the storm god, when he was killed by his enemies. In the story of Baal, Baal and his enemies fight for control over the world. The alternating dominance of each god was expressed by the alternation of fertility and infertility in the agricultural year. But Yahweh does not suffer periodic defeat at the hands of his divine enemies. His cosmogonic victory has established the entire universe once and for all. Therefore mourning can never be part of his official ritual.

The emphasis in v. 2 should fall on "the Lord." The people belong to the Lord who holds absolute sovereignty forever; there are no other powerful gods in the universe. Behind v. 2 is the view that other nations may have their heavenly patrons, all under Yahweh of course, but Israel is the Lord's own people, "holy to the Lord." The word for "his own possession," *segulla,* is a term found also in international law. The cognate word describes the subject of the Hittite king in connection with his duties as vassal: acknowledging his lord, performing the prescribed visits to the sovereign's court. Other texts describe the relation of a wife to her husband with the same term. Here the term is approximately parallel to "holy," defining further the especially close relation of the people to their Lord.

Ancient peoples were much concerned with classification of natural phenomena, and vv. 3-20 is an instance of such preoccupation. It is not clear whether certain animals were excluded on the grounds that they were toxic or on the grounds that they were used in the rituals of neighboring peoples. The criteria of cloven-foot and of chewing the cud may have been developed from observation of just a few permitted and prohibited animals, the theory later being derived from a few particular cases. At any rate, the list begins with clean land animals, excluding those which do not meet the two criteria of hoof and cud (vv. 3-8). Next, sea creatures are dealt with (vv. 9-10), birds (vv. 11-18), and finally, winged insects (v. 19). Verse 21 forbids what has died of itself to be eaten by the Israelite but permits it to the resident alien and the sale of it to the foreigner. No explanation is given but the prohibition may arise from considerations of public health, or because the blood would not have been properly poured out according to law (cf., 12:16, 23-25). The prohibition against boiling a kid in its mother's milk is mysterious. There is no clear evidence that it was part of a Canaanite ritual.

Moses is convinced that the people's holiness is grounded in their nearness to the Lord of all the world. They are to be aware of their apartness, and avoid all foods which would diminish their special state.

SACRED DUES FROM A RICH LAND
14:22—15:23

²²"You shall tithe all the yield of your seed, which comes forth from the field year by year. ²³And before the Lord your God, in the place which he will choose, to make his name dwell there, you shall eat the tithe of your grain, of your wine, and of your oil, and the firstlings of your herd and flock; that you may learn to fear the Lord your God always.

²⁸"At the end of every three years you shall bring forth all the tithe of your produce in the same year, and lay it up within your towns; ²⁹and the Levite, because he has no portion or inheritance with you, and the sojourner, the fatherless, and the widow, who are within your towns, shall come and eat and be filled; that the Lord your God may bless you in all the work of your hands that you do.

15 "At the end of every seven years you shall grant a release. ²And this is the manner of the release: every creditor shall release what he has lent to his neighbor; he shall not exact it of his neighbor, his brother, because the Lord's release has been proclaimed. ³Of a foreigner you may exact it; but whatever of yours is with your brother your hand shall release. ⁴But there will be no poor among you (for the Lord will bless you in the land which the Lord your God gives you for an inheritance to possess), ⁵if only you will obey the voice of the Lord your God, being careful to do all this commandment which I command you this day. ⁶For the Lord your God will bless you, as he promised you, and you shall lend to many nations, but you shall not borrow; and you shall rule over many nations, but they shall not rule over you.

¹²"If your brother, a Hebrew man, or a Hebrew woman, is sold to you, he shall serve you six years, and in the seventh year you shall let him go free from you. ¹³And when you let him go free from you, you shall not let him go empty-handed; ¹⁴you shall furnish him liberally out of your flock, out of your threshing floor, and out of your wine press; as the Lord your God has blessed you, you shall give to him. ¹⁵You shall remember that you were a slave in the land of Egypt, and the Lord your God redeemed you; therefore I command you this today.

¹⁹"All the firstling males that are born of your herd and flock you shall consecrate to the Lord your God; you shall do no work with the firstling of your herd, nor shear the firstling of your flock. ²⁰You shall eat it, you and your household, before the Lord your God year by year at the place which the Lord will choose."

The section deals with a single theme, the distribution of the rich bounty of the land, whether to the Lord in tithes and firstlings, or to fellow Israelites in the sharing of those same tithes and firstlings; and the provision for the periodic release of debts and of bondage. The sections are easily discerned: 14:22-27, the annual tithe; 14:28-29, the triennial tithe; 15:1-6, the year of release of debts; 15:7-11, special provision for the poor in the year of release; 15:12-18, the release of slaves; and 15:19-23, firstlings of the flock and herd.

The practice of tithing or giving a tenth to the god was

widely practiced in antiquity, especially in regard to the produce of the soil. The practice apparently reflects the belief that the land belongs to the gods and a gift betokening the whole was to be made in acknowledgment of blessings and for future prosperity. Often the tithe was given to the temple staff to pay for temple expenses. And in the East, the sovereign often took a considerable portion of the tithe for himself.

Only against this background can the Deuteronomic perspective be appreciated. Here the tithe is not directed toward the maintenance of temple or palace but toward the enjoyment of the offerer and his household, and the third-year tithe is for the sustenance of the poor and needy within Israel. This humane concern of Deuteronomy is at variance as well with biblical custom, particularly the customs in the Priestly Code. In Num 18:21-28 of the Priestly Code the tithe is given over entirely to the priestly tribe—to the Levites first, and then a tenth of that to the priests. In Deuteronomy, the Levites receive their due only as members of the poor class (14:29). This brief commentary offers no solution to the difficult problem of the tithe in Deuteronomy and the Priestly Code. Any discussion of the problem however has to take into account the different intentions of each work—the Priestly Code's exclusive focus on priestly life and the Deuteronomists' aim to interpret ancient customs for a lay audience. The Deuteronomist naturally will emphasize the meaning of the rite for all Israel—that it is an occasion for appreciating the varied produce of the land and for rejoicing with one's household. Deuteronomy will also adjust the practice of tithing to the law of a single sanctuary.

The peculiarly Deuteronomic stamp seen already in 14:22-29 is even more conspicuous in the law concerning the release of indebtedness in 15:1-11. The old legislation in Exod 23:10-11 and the Priestly Code in Lev 25:1-7 spoke only of letting the land lie fallow every seventh year "that the poor of your people may eat" (Exod 23:11) and the land may rest. Deuteronomy extends care for the poor much further—to the release of their debts. So strong is his faith in the land's ability adequately to support every Israelite that he states there will be no poor people at all if the people are truly obedient.

The distinctiveness of this chapter's teaching on Hebrew slaves can be seen by comparing 15:12-18 with the old legislation in Exod 21:2-11. In Deut 15:13-15, the master is to set up the freed slave's household from the remembrance "that you yourself were once a slave in the land of Egypt" (v. 15). The master is to reflect how much is owed to the slave; these are humane considerations designed to ease the ex-slave's lot. In addition, Deuteronomy places the female slave on the same footing as the male in vv. 12 and 17, an advance over Exod 21.

The direction to the Israelite to eat the firstlings with the entire household is likewise a Deuteronomic shift. In Num 18:15-18, the firstlings are assigned to Aaron, i.e. to the priests, with the words, "And their flesh shall be thine," instead of being eaten by the owner and his household at the central sanctuary.

The review of these and other details will show the peculiar stamp that the laws have been given in this book. This commentary does not want to suggest that the discrepancies between the Priestly Code and Deuteronomy can be totally explained by saying Deuteronomy has turned old law into relevant preaching. The situation is too complex for such a simple solution. One has, for example, to reckon with historical development and variety of practice. But nonetheless the homiletic and popular character of Deuteronomy remains a powerful shaper of old traditions.

Regarding the details of 14:22-27, chap. 12 has already stated that all public ritual such as tithings must take place in the central sanctuary. The very process of offering the produce of a rich land and sharing it with one's household is educative—one learns the meaning of the great commandment as one experiences the life latent in the land (14:23). Verses 24-26 in chap. 14 accommodate tithing to the law of the single sanctuary. One cannot carry ten percent of the produce all the way to Jerusalem but one can easily carry the monetary equivalent and change it back into food for feasting in the central shrine.

The triennial tithe (vv. 28-29) is entirely given away to the poor—a unique Deuteronomic touch. It is not brought to the sanctuary, but stored in the towns, presumably for periodic distribution. The bounty of the land is scattered to the poor by this device—a beautiful gesture. The distribution of the tithe to the Levites is related to the custom in Num 18:21-28 where the tithes are given to the priests.

The release of debts every seventh year (15:1-11) is, as has been noted, the expansion of the principle of letting the land rest every seventh year. Is the custom a cancellation of all debts or only the suspension, for one year, of the creditor's right to demand payment? Jewish tradition holds that it is a cancellation. The majority view, however, holds the second, that it is a postponement of payment, a postponement understandable in the weakening of the economy that would take place with fields fallow in the same year. Commercial loans in the modern sense were not a practice. Individuals generally borrowed for the relief of some temporary difficulty or impoverishment.

The same attitude toward the potential bounty of the land as has been seen under tithes is also evident in vv. 4-6. These verses most probably mean that ideally the land will provide so much that there will be no poor at all—if Israel is obedient. Israel's prosperity among the nations (v. 6) will reflect the Lord's preeminence in the world. If Israel were truly obedient there would be no poor and hence no need for borrowing (given the ancient custom that one borrows only in distress).

Verses 7-11, in countering the natural tendency of the lender not to make loans close to the year of release, provides beautiful vocabulary and concepts of generosity— "do not harden your heart"; "do not close your hand away from your poor brother"; "open your hand." The reason for not calculating times is that there will always be poor among the people (v. 11).

Slaves of Hebrew origin were relatively well cared for in law. The slave, either male or female, was to be freed in the seventh year of service. The master is told to set up the slave with some possessions. The liberal treatment of the ex-slave is to arise from the master's consciousness that he too is a freed slave (vv. 14b-15). The rhythm of redemption, slavery and freedom in one's land, is to be re-experienced by the master as he watches his own slave come to freedom and independence. If the slave prefers to stay with the master—quite possibly because the slave's spouse and children might still belong to the master—then the slave can so declare and be perpetually bonded.

The last section, 15:19-23, deals with the firstlings, stipulating that they, like the tithes of the soil, are to be eaten in the place which the Lord chooses. The first born belongs in a special way to the Lord who opens all wombs. As a sacral act of returning the animal to the Lord, the eating must be done in the Lord's sanctuary. Here again, the bounty of the land is emphasized more than fulfillment of ritual. If the animal is blemished it cannot, of course, be offered to the Lord, and so is to be eaten as if it were wild game, and in any place.

There are few passages in Deuteronomy where the wondrous power of the Lord's land to provide for the people is so beautifully and consistently articulated. It is truly the land on which Israel is to live -- in abundance and in sharing with the poor.

THE PILGRIMAGE FEASTS
16:1-17

> **16** "Three times a year all your males shall appear before the Lord your God at the place which he will choose: at the feast of unleavened bread, at the feast of weeks, and at the feast of booths. They shall not appear before the Lord empty-handed; [17]every man shall give as he is able, according to the blessing of the Lord your God which he has given you."

The section on sacred dues, just examined, emphasizes the bounty of the land and ensures that the bounty be distributed as widely as possible and be the cause of festive rejoicing. At the same time, historical memory is to inform every Israelite that he or she is a freed slave (15:15). In 16:1-17, the calendar of the annual pilgrimage feast, one finds the same celebration of the fertile life of the land but with an even more pronounced emphasis on the memory of the historical events that made possible their presence on the land. Each feast celebrates an aspect of the exodus-conquest. Passover is celebrated in the same month as the flight from Egypt and the unleavened bread recalls the flight, too hurried for leaven to be put into the flour for baking bread. The Feast of Weeks is an occasion for remembering their slave status (v. 12). One ought not, however, to exaggerate the historical consciousness in Israel as it celebrated the three feasts, especially in Deuteronomy. The account of the Feast of Tabernacles in this chapter mentions nothing of the wilderness period of tent dwelling. Celebration of the fertility of the land is paramount, though of course the land is seen as the gift of the Lord and the goal of the exodus-conquest.

The three feasts at which all males were to present themselves to the Lord at his sanctuary—males were representing the entire family (cf. 16:11, "you and your son and your daughter, your manservant and your maidservant," etc.)—were ancient institutions in Israel. They appear in all the main biblical traditions, in the old epic source (also called J-E), e.g., Exod 23:14-17; 34:18, 22-23; and, with considerable detail, in the various currents of the Priestly tradition, Leviticus 23 and Numbers 28-29. The Deuteronomic version of the calendar characteristically insists on localization in the central sanctuary and, in the case of the Feasts of Weeks and Booths, on the joyousness and hospitality to be shown a the sacred meal there. Deuteronomy as usual amplifies the old tradition.

The Passover regulations, 16:1-8, combine into one the passover sacrifice of an animal (sheep or oxen here as against the lamb of the Priestly Code) with the rite of unleavened bread. The other traditions keep the two rites distinct. Celebration is to be on the anniversary of the departure from Egypt. After the animal sacrifice, unleavened bread is to be eaten for seven days. Verses 4 and 5 repeat in reverse order vv. 2-3, a sign of the homiletic nature of the passage. The rite, as sacred, must be celebrated in the central sanctuary. In the old tradition regarding Passover, e.g. Exod 12:21-27, the feast had a domestic character which is lost in Deuteronomy.

It is generally agreed among scholars that the Passover sacrifice, a sheep or oxen in Deuteronomy, a lamb in the Priestly tradition, was originally at home among herders, perhaps part of the process of breaking camp and heading for new pastures. The elimination of all leaven, on the other hand, was a rite originally of farmers. The idea was apparently to get rid of the leaven of the previous year and to start afresh, a kind of spring cleaning of the larder. The two rites, one relating to flocks and herds and the other to the produce of the soil, have been combined by the Israelites and, without loss of their agricultural meaning, have become the bearers of the historical memory of Israel's beginnings in Egypt. In their celebration the Israelites remember liturgically the great deeds of old which have brought them into existence—the Lord's freeing them from slavery, his leading them in the wilderness, and his presence among them through the fertility of the land. One should not oppose historical memory to agricultural experience in these feasts; the land is to be seen always as the goal of the exodus-conquest and hence as part of the national story.

Verses 9-12 deal with the Feast of Weeks, so named for the manner of reckoning it—from the beginning of the wheat harvest. Deuteronomy makes no allusion to first fruits, a central concern of this feast in the other traditions. The donation is a freewill offering—according to the discretion of the individual. All are to enjoy the feast, the Levite and the poor along with the family of the offerer. So the memory of Israel's former servitude will be honored. Not endowed with land the Levite is ranked among the typically poor—the fatherless and the widow; each can make a special claim upon the Lord and fellow Israelites.

The Feast of Booths, vv. 13-15, is so named because during the octave of this feast the people lived in temporary huts made of boughs, a vestige probably of the temporary field dwellings of harvesters. This detail has been "historicized" to signify the ancestors' dwelling in tents in the wilderness. It was the most popular and most widely observed of the feasts, sometimes being called simply "the feast." The significance of the feast is clear from its name in the epic tradition, "the Feast of Ingathering." The "ingathering" was chiefly of grapes, olives, dates, and figs which were harvested in the late summer. The time was held to be "the turning of the year," i.e., when the old year ended and the new year of fertility began (the rain began again about this time). Thanks were given for the produce of the year and also for the return of fertilizing rains. Deuteronomy makes this feast entirely celebratory of the land's yield, omitting the note, found in other traditions, that the booths recall the tents of the wilderness period.

Verses 16-17, reprinted above, sum up the calendar. By their demand that all Israelites appear before the Lord in his sanctuary the verses underscore the pilgrimage nature of the celebration. The feast was not simply a religious feast like our Christmas or Easter but was like the Islamic *ḥaj* (the same word as the Hebrew word for feast), that great annual pilgrimage to Mecca which every Moslem must go on, a festival consisting of a pilgrimage to a sanctuary. The central sanctuary was to be the site of a holy exchange between the Lord and his people—the people returning to the Lord the gifts he himself has given. In this arena of abundance, no one is to appear without gifts, "empty-handed."

With these prescriptions, Moses sanctifies the seasons of the year. Privileged moments are provided for the people to gather together before the Lord—to recount the story of how they became the Lord's people and to enjoy together the bounty of the land in its seasonal yield.

OFFICIALS IN ISRAEL. BALANCE OF POWERS AND SUBORDINATION TO THE WRITTEN LAW. 16:18—18:22

16 [18]"You shall appoint judges and officers in all your towns which Lord your God gives you, according to your tribes; and they shall judge the people with righteous judgment. [19]You shall not pervert justice; you shall not show partiality; and you shall not take a bribe, for a bribe blinds the eyes of the wise and subverts the cause of the righteous. [20]Justice, and only justice, you shall follow, that you may live and inherit the land which the Lord your God gives you.

17 [14]"When you come to the land which the Lord your God gives you, and you possess it and dwell in it, and then say, 'I will set a king over me, like all the nations that are round about me'; [15]you may indeed set as king over you him whom the Lord your God will choose. One from among your brethren you shall set as king over you; you may not put a foreigner over you, who is not your brother.

[18]"And when he sits on the throne of his kingdom, he shall write for himself in a book a copy of this law, from that which is in charge of the Levitical priests; [19]and it shall be with him, and he shall read in it all the days of his life, that he may learn to fear the Lord his God, by keeping all the words of this law and these statutes, and doing them; [20]that his heart may not be lifted up above his brethren, and that he may not turn aside from the commandment, either to the right hand or to the left; so that he may continue long in his kingdom, he and his children, in Israel.

18 "The Levitical priests, that is, all the tribe of Levi, shall have no portion or inheritance with Israel; they shall eat the offerings by fire to the Lord, and his rightful dues. ²They shall have no inheritance among their brethren; the Lord is their inheritance, as he promised them.

⁹"When you come into the land which the Lord your God gives you, you shall not learn to follow the abominable practices of those nations. ¹⁰There shall not be found among you any one who burns his son or his daughter as an offering," any one who practices divination, a soothsayer, or an augur, or a sorcerer, ¹¹or a charmer, or a medium, or a wizard, or a necromancer. ¹²For whoever does these things is an abomination to the Lord; and because of these abominable practices the Lord your God is driving them out before you. ¹³You shall be blameless before the Lord your God. ¹⁴For these nations, which you are about to dispossess, give heed to soothsayers and to diviners; but as for you, the Lord your God has not allowed you so to do.

¹⁵"The Lord your God will raise up for you a prophet like me from among you, from your brethren—him you shall heed—¹⁶just as you desired of the Lord your God at Horeb on the day of the assembly, when you said, 'Let me not hear again the voice of the Lord my God, or see this great fire any more, lest I die.' ¹⁷And the Lord said to me, 'They have rightly said all that they have spoken. ¹⁸I will raise up for them a prophet like you from among their brethren; and I will put my words in his mouth, and he shall speak to them all that I command him.' "

Deuteronomy 16:18 with its mention of judges and officials introduces a lengthy section on the governance of the people in the new land: the magistrates and officials, 16:18—17:13; the king, 17:14-20; the Levitical priests, 18:1-8; the prophet, 18:9-22. The section may seem an abrupt shift from the liturgical laws of chaps. 12-16 with their concern for a single sanctuary, exclusivity of worship of the Lord, clean and unclean food, and sacral duties. They are not. Ancient societies did not distinguish sharply between sacred and secular rulers. The authority structure of a society was divinely ordained even in minor details; kingship as well as other aspects of governance was from the gods.

Though the divine origin of offices in Israel was not exceptional in the ancient Near East, the balance of powers implicit in the carefully separated branches of governance—judicial, liturgical, royal, and prophetic—and the subjection of the king to a written law, was without ancient parallel. To bring out the first point, one needs to show that the whole section of 16:18-18:22 has been deliberately edited from a single point of view. One can admit that its individual elements are not of the same antiquity or origin. But there are signs of a single consistent point of view. One indication of editorial unity is the A-B-A sequence in 16:18—19:21 that is found elsewhere in Deuteronomy, e.g., chap. 8, and frequently in Hebrew rhetoric. The first section, A, is 16:18—17:13 concerning the judicial process which is echoed in 19:1-21, A , again about the judicial process. In particular, 19:15-21, concerning witnesses, echoes 17:6-7. The persons mentioned in 16:18—17:13, magistrate, officials, and priest, suggest the themes of "king," "priest," and "prophet." In this section, the installation of judges in 16:18—17:13 serves both as introduction to the group of officials in chaps. 17 and 18 and also to the legal institutions of chaps. 19 forward. Thus the chapters belong together. Another indicator of editorial unity is the mention of the written copy of the law in 17:18, which can only refer to Deuteronomy 15-26. It implies that the whole section was seen as a unity.

If it be true that this section is an editorial unity, the editor is affirming that no single office can be understood apart from the others. The king's role, for example, can only be appreciated against that of the priest, "[the king] shall write for himself in a book a copy of this law from that which is in charge of the Levitical priests" (17:18). Not only is the power of each official defined and circumscribed by the power of the other—an ancient instance of Montesquieu's theory of balance of powers (so Norbert Lohfink)—the authority of each one is also under the written law. Though the latter point is made explicitly only with regard to the king in 17:18, it is true for all.

It is time to examine the individual offices, first the judges and their work (16:18—17:13). Magistrates are to be appointed by Israel (probably by the elders of the tribes) "in all your towns," a Deuteronomic phrase used for a plurality of places in opposition to the unique central sanctuary. Like chap. 12, some actions take place "in any of your towns" (16:18; cf. 12:15, 21) and others in "the place which the Lord your God will choose" (17:18; cf. 12:5, 11). The court in the central sanctuary of 17:8-13 is not an appeals court for the local courts. It functions alongside them, trying technically difficult cases (17:8).

Some scholars mistakenly deny unity to the passage about judges and assert that 16:21-17:1 about cultic prohibitions are intrusive. In reality, the entire passage is developed largely through imperatives such as one finds also in the disputed verses; the commands show what is ideally typical and illustrate how the judicial process is to operate. Verses 16-20, the strong prohibition against partiality and bribery, was doubly necessary in a culture where officials were popularly expected to profit from their administrative positions. On the contrary, Israel's very well-being depends on the impartial carrying out of justice (16:20b).

Sample concerns of the local magistrates are found in 16:21—17:1, essentially violations of the first commandment through introduction of "abominations" or cultic irregularities like sacred trees or pillars into the worship of the Lord. "Secular" cases were undoubtedly heard in these courts as one infers from 17:8 which implies that the local courts could hear uncomplicated cases of homicide, civil law, and assault. But in keeping with the Deuteronomist's concern for true worship and liturgical correctness, the samples chosen concern the great commandment. Another sample of violation of the great commandment, "transgression of the covenant," is given in 17:2-7 which provides regulations on dealing with witnesses. Heavenly bodies, then as now credited with earthly influence, were often thought to be a deity's manner of self-presentation. The worshipper of the heavenly bodies is to be sentenced to death and the hand of the informant is to cast the first stone. All the people are to join in the purgation of the abomination from Israel's midst.

The court in Jerusalem, 17:8-13, presided over both by Levitical priests and lay judges (17:9, 12), considers the complex cases. Emphasis is laid upon the obedience due the *torah* or legal decision (*RSV* "instructions" of v. 11). There is no doubt about the authority of the central court. Disobedience is punishable by death.

Since in the East the king was the chief judicial officer, he is dealt with in the section after the judges, 17:14-20. What is truly extraordinary is that the king is not mentioned at all in the section on judges. Not only is he deprived of his customary place in the legal system, he is also deprived of the other customary role of a king—leadership of a standing army. Deuteronomy distinguishes between the king's own troops which he may lead but not enlarge beyond measure (17:16) and the large army which is under "the priest" and "the officials," in 20:1-9. With the king so limited in power, it is not surprising that the chapter views positively the popular demand for a king (17:14-15). Conditions are established even beyond the limits mentioned above. The king must be an Israelite; he must be chosen by the Lord, i.e. the dynasty must be founded by divine choice. The king is not to build up excessively his army (measured in cavalry), nor should he engage in dynastic marriages which introduce foreign wives and their own national gods into the palace.

Most striking of all the king's duties is that he read regularly from the law, i.e. Deuteronomy 5-28. The reason given is the same as would apply to any Israelite—that he may learn to be absolutely faithful to the Lord in all the circumstances of his life. On his obedience to the law depends the survival of his dynasty. The king by sharing his power with priest, judge and prophet, and by his obedience to the law does not conform to ancient Near Eastern royalty but becomes a model Israelite.

Deuteronomy 18:1-8 describes the priests in a seemingly odd way—by the revenues in kind due to them. Mention of the sacral revenues in vv. 3-8 however is just another way of stating the divine institution of the priests. The Lord has not given to the tribe of Levi any "portion or inheritance," i.e., a grant of land from which to draw their livelihood. Their sustenance will come from things dedicated to the Lord, edibles which have been transferred into the sacred sphere, or sacrificed. Since the Lord is their heritage, they may eat of the food which belongs to the Lord.

The interpretation of the Levites in Deuteronomy (D) differs sharply from that in the Priestly Code (P). Their revenues are described differently as has been seen already under 14:27, 29 where the Levite in Deuteronomy receives much smaller dues in tithes, firstlings and sacrifices than in P, and on a different basis. In P, 48 cities are allotted to the tribe of Levi (Num 35:1-8 and Joshua 21), whereas in Deuteronomy they are homeless and destitute. The very definition of "Levite" is different in the two traditions. In P it denotes the members of the tribe, *exclusive* of the priests who are called rather the descendants of Aaron. In Deuteronomy it denotes *all* members of the tribe without distinction. There is a distinction between "priest" and "Levite" in both D and P. For P the priests are a fixed minority of the entire tribe, only the descendants of Aaron. For D, the priests are a fluctuating minority, the members of the tribe who happen to be officiating at a particular time. It may be that D represents an early stage before specialization, and in fact by its affirming the rights of country Levites D is trying to maintain the old understanding as opportunities for functioning as priests diminish with the reduction of sanctuaries to a single place of worship.

At any rate the entire section assigns to the priests three

functions: pronouncing of legal decisions or *torah* at the central court (17:9, 12); offering sacrifice from which he may take his due (18:1-8); guarding and teaching the law (17:18). The third task is emphasized in 31:9-13.

Priestly power in its turn is limited. In early times the priests through their manipulation of Urim and Thummim, the casting of sacred lots, put the worshipper directly in touch with the will of God. Here the function of speaking forth the contemporary meaning of the Lord is not to be exercised by the priests but by the prophets, the last of the officials to be discussed, in 18:9-22.

Prophecy is the Israelite alternative to the abominable practices of the Canaanites. As in chap. 7 and especially in chap. 12, the corrupt practices in the worship of the many Canaanite gods cannot be the basis of worship appropriate to the one Lord of Israel. The Lord will not reveal himself through the manipulation of professionals but only through the charismatic prophet, called by the Lord.

The prophet is directly called by God and his message is rooted in the Horeb (Sinai) experience when Israel encountered its God. The plea of the people at that time that there be a mediator, and the Lord's acceptance of that plea, is the basis for the "office" of charismatic prophet. The prophet makes actual or contemporary the words of the law. His words are to be obeyed as the words of God. Conversely, anyone presumptuous enough to speak as a prophet without being called is to die. Contact with the divine will is through the prophet who continues in every age Moses' task of proclaiming and interpreting the law. This understanding of prophet makes it possible for later Israel to hear the speeches of Deuteronomy, some of which are late, as the words of Moses.

The Deuteronomic editing is concerned on the one hand with interpreting the various offices in Israel as a balance of powers, and on the other, to show that all offices are ordered toward a single reality, the written law. Each office is differently balanced and ordered. The law which comes from Horeb is entrusted to the priests for safekeeping and for teaching. It is interpreted as a living document by the prophets who expand and complete it according to the needs of each age. The king, like every other Israelite, is to live according to this law. The judges are to judge according to its principles.

THE ADMINISTRATION OF JUSTICE
19:1-21 (cont. from 16:18—17:13)

19 "When the Lord your God cuts off the nations whose land the Lord your God gives you, and you dispossess them and dwell in their cities and in their houses, ²you shall set apart three cities for you in the land which the Lord your God gives you to possess. ³You shall prepare the roads, and divide into three parts the area of the land which the Lord your God gives you as a possession, so that any manslayer can flee to them.

¹⁴"In the inheritance which you will hold in the land that the Lord your God gives you to possess, you shall not remove your neighbor's landmark, which the men of old have set.

¹⁵"A single witness shall not prevail against a man for any crime or for any wrong in connection with any offense that he has committed; only on the evidence of two witnesses, or of three witnesses, shall a charge be sustained. . . . ²¹Your eye shall not pity; it shall be life for life, eye for eye, tooth for tooth, hand for hand, foot for foot."

It has been pointed out already that chap. 19, which is concerned with judicial matters, especially valid witnesses, is connected to 16:18-17:13 in an A-B-A´ pattern. A and A´ stand for material on justice and B stands for what has been inserted in between (material on the other officials). The structure is also called chiasm, from the Greek letter *chi* or X. The earlier section, A, has already introduced the local magistrates and officials, the Levitical priests and lay judges in the central court; these will administer the laws of chap. 19.

In Transjordan Moses instituted the cities of refuge, Bezer, Ramoth, and Golan (4:41-43). The three cities here, with provision for three more as Israel expands its territory (v. 9), are not named since in the perspective of the speech the Israelites have not yet settled the land.

The underlying concern of the several laws—the use and abuse of cities of refuge, the non-removal of ancient landmarks, the rule of witnesses—is to safeguard the sacredness of the land. The first law, about the cities of refuge (the phrase is actually not from Deuteronomy but from the Priestly Code), takes effect only after the conquest and settlement in the land (vv. 1-2). Only then will the land be fully purged of the malicious influence of the nations and their gods. The Lord then will have led his people definitively into the land which is his by conquest. The allotment of land, detailed in Joshua 13-21, is simply an extension of the power of the conquest. The city of refuge for the protection of the person who does not deserve to die is a device for preventing the spilling of innocent blood and the consequent pollution of the sacred land. And protection of ancient boundary stones preserves the original boundaries of the tribes as they were assigned to the tribes (v. 14).

The law provides that only accidental killers may take advantage of the cities. They are not for cases of premeditated killing (vv. 11-13). Presumably the killer fled to the city as soon as possible after the accident, explaining the circumstances to the local judges (16:18) or to the elders (19:12) to whom was granted the right of admittance.

The "avenger of blood" is the nearest kinsman of the person who was killed. In ancient custom, he had the right and duty to avenge the blood, or death, of his relative. Blood shed wrongfully calls for justice. The Lord says to Cain regarding Abel's murder, "The voice of your brother's blood is crying to me from the ground" (Gen 4:10). In modern societies, the right of punishment is the state's; not so in Hebrew and in many other societies. The private avenger (Heb. *gō'ēl*, often translated "redeemer" when used of the Lord), and not the state exacted punishment. Hebrew law also demands that wilful murder be atoned for by the blood of the murderer, and not by any form of payment. "The elders of his town shall hand him [the murderer] over to the blood avenger to be put to death; you must show him no pity. Thus you will purge Israel of the blood of the innocent, and it will go well with you" (vv. 12-13). Hence the city of refuge controls untrammeled private vengeance, "lest innocent blood be shed in your land. . . and so the guilt of bloodshed be upon you" (v. 10).

The respect due ancient boundaries in v. 14 is another instance of the respect for the holiness of the land, i.e., that the land is the Lord's and its allotment belongs to him. Removal of the marker of those boundaries is a severe disturbance to the integrity of the Lord's initial grant.

Verses 15-21, like 17:6-7, treats of witnesses, stating the need of two or more for validity. The first passage deals with witnesses of idolatry. Here the same rule is extended to any crime (v. 15). The difficult case of a false witness is to be taken to the central court described in 17:8-13. The phrase "before the Lord" usually means in Deuteronomy "in the central shrine." There, before the priests and the lay judges, the matter is to be settled. Ordeals existed for determining the truth or falsehood of statements when no independent checks were available. But the text does not describe the means used here—probably because the emphasis of the text falls not on the ordeal itself but on the punishment. The lying witness is to undergo the very evil he or she meant to inflict. That the devices of the wicked often return upon their own head is a commonplace of Hebrew thought. The punishment of the false witness illustrates the axiom perfectly.

The final statement of the chapter, "Your eye shall not

pity; it shall be life for life, eye for eye, tooth for tooth, hand for hand, foot for foot," disturbs many modern readers who blame the seemingly harsh practice upon a harsh God. In its context, however, the principle of equality of punishment actually moderates uncontrolled vengeance by the relatives of injured persons. In cases of only physical injury the avenger was not to kill but only to exact an equivalent loss—e.g. an eye for an eye. There was no prison system. Punishment for violence had to be swift and decisive, and such as to provide a lesson for others (v. 20). The principle of talion, *lex talionis* in Latin, becomes in this part of the chapter a principle of equivalent punishment. The lying witness is to suffer what he or she intended for the victim.

The chapter shows that the land granted by the Lord is to be honored by exemplary behavior and respect for the original gift.

HOLY WAR ON BEHALF OF THE LAND
20:1-20

20 "When you go forth to war against your enemies, and see horses and chariots and an army larger than your own, you shall not be afraid of them; for the Lord your God is with you, who brought you up out of the land of Egypt. ²And when you draw near to the battle, the priest shall come forward and speak to the people, ³and shall say to them, 'Hear, O Israel, you draw near this day to battle against your enemies: let not your heart faint; do not fear, or tremble, or be in dread of them; ⁴for the Lord your God is he that goes with you, to fight for you against your enemies, to give you the victory.' ⁵Then the officers shall speak to the people, saying, 'What man is there that has built a new house and has not dedicated it? Let him go back to his house, lest he die in the battle and another man dedicate it. ⁶And what man is there that has planted a vineyard and has not enjoyed its fruit? Let him go back to his house, lest he die in the battle and another man enjoy its fruit. [7]And what man is there that has betrothed a wife and has not taken her? Let him go back to his house, lest he die in the battle and another man take her.'

[10]"When you draw near to a city to fight against it, offer terms of peace to it. [11]And if its answer to you is peace and it opens to you, then all the people who are found in it shall do forced labor for you and shall serve you. [12]But if it makes no peace with you, but makes war against you, then you shall besiege it:

[19]"When you besiege a city for a long time, making war against it in order to take it, you shall not destroy its trees by wielding an axe against them; for you may eat of them, but you shall not cut them down.

Chapter 7 is the other chapter in the book which deals with war against the seven nations occupying the land which Israel is to possess. In 20:17 "the Girgashites" is to be added to the six nations listed in the *RSV*, following the evidence of the Greek text. Both chapters inculcate a severe attitude toward the predecessors of Israel in the land; the nations are a threat to Israel's fidelity to their Lord. Chapter 7, like the other sermons in chaps. 5-11, is principally concerned with inculcating the Great Commandment. The Israelites are to eradicate any nation that would teach them to worship the gods of the land. Chapter 20 shows similar concern for purity of worship in the land (vv. 16-18), but it mainly deals with the means of defending the land—holy war. Verses 1-9 are about the attitude of the warriors shown through a sampling of the speeches delivered just prior to combat; vv. 10-18 are about the treatment of defeated enemies; and vv. 19-20 provide for the protection of fruit trees in time of war.

The topic of holy war has already been treated under chaps. 1-3 and 7. Briefly, holy war was thought to be carried out on two levels: the heavenly sphere where the gods of the warring nations engaged in a struggle for power, and the earthly plane where the nations actually fought. Since the fate of the nations was linked to the outcome of the heavenly struggle, priests and prophets who could announce the progress and outcome of the heavenly scene had a role to play in the ritual of war. In the case of Israel, its belief that there was only one powerful deity, their own Yahweh, inevitably led to the conviction that victory was theirs if they were on the Lord's side. Their task would then be to go into battle with the firm conviction that the enemy was in their hands. They were to trust in their Divine Warrior who had shown his power in their regard in the classic battle against Pharaoh and in the conquest (v. 1). The little sermons here, probably literary digests of actual military exhortations, speak of the confidence Israel is to have in the power of its Lord both in the heavenly and earthly worlds, "for the Lord is he that goes with you, to fight for you against your enemies, to give you the victory" (v. 4). All those whom ancient custom temporarily excused from service (vv. 5-7) are to go home and, even more important, all those who are unable to draw courage from the presence of the Lord with the army (vv. 8-9).

On the assumption that war led by the Lord with Israel's faithful participation always ended in victory, the next section deals with the treatment of conquered enemies. With enemies defeated in "cities which are very far from you" (v. 15), i.e., outside the boundaries of the holy land, Israel may enter into a vassal treaty ("offer terms of peace" in v. 10). If the city does not wish to enter into a treaty, all the people are to be slaughtered and their property becomes the property of Israel. In regard to populations within Canaan, no treaties are to be made since they with their foreign gods pose a continual temptation to infidelity. They are to be annihilated, the seven nations by their number expressing the totality of previous inhabitants.

Even the little coda in vv. 19-20, odd as it may seem, reflects a care for the defense of the land in time of war. The great powers, particularly Egypt, laid waste enemy lands as as matter of policy. Israel is not to do so since that would interfere with the fertility of the holy land. Fruit trees are not to be cut down at all to provide wood for seige engines.

An examination of some of the details supports the above interpretation. In v. 1, "horses and chariots" are of course cavalry, a specialized and expensive branch of an army that Israel often lacked. "An army larger than your own" is in apposition to "horses and chariots." Israel is to remember the Lord of the exodus who showed himself to be a warrior in battle with Pharaoh's troops. The two officials of vv. 2-9 were already introduced in the prior section; the priest in 17:12, 18; 18:1-8, and the officers in 16:18. Their role in war is mentioned for the first time here. Some scholars have seen in the priest's exhortation not to fear the enemy because the Lord has gone before, to be an important paradigm for understanding faith elsewhere in the Old Testament. Faith in the savior Lord comes to fullest expression when the believer trusts the Lord will battle against the onrushing enemy.

The officials in vv. 5-9 exempt from service certain categories, e.g. recruits who have not yet enjoyed full status as adults shown in such acts as ownership of one's own house (as opposed to living with less than full independence at one's parent's house). "Dedicated" in v. 5 is to be rendered "and has not lived in it." Verse 7, "Is there anyone who has not paid the bride-price for a wife and has not yet married her?" The officers further try to rid the army of the cowards (v. 8) whose panic might spread to the whole army in the heat of combat. In the battles of the time, panic could determine the outcome. The army, reduced only to those who believe the Lord goes before them, is now placed in the charge of its officers (v. 9).

Victory is assured in an authentic war of the Lord and so the case of the captured populations has to be considered. The disposal of prisoners of war in an age that could not support prison camps was a problem. Distant cities not posing a threat to Israel can get off with vassal status.

Resisting cities are to be destroyed. So also all the near cities—placed under the ban of holy war.

A touch of Deuteronomic "humanism" is to be found in the last two verses of the chapter protecting the trees. Verse 20 is best translated, "Are trees of the field human beings likely to withdraw before you into the besieged city?" No one is to trifle with the fertility of the land.

The chapter by recasting old exhortations of holy war teaches Israel how it is to conduct itself before any threat—by trusting in the Lord who goes before.

Chapters 21-25 contain a wide variety of laws, with less characteristic Deuteronomic exhortation than has appeared in the chapters so far. They are all concerned with Israel's conduct in the land, how it is to express its identity as the Lord's people. Because the laws are so brief and independent, this commentary will comment on them grouped somewhat artificially according to chapter numeration rather than topically.

LAWS OF UNSOLVED MURDER, FAIR TREATMENT OF WOMEN, REBELLIOUS CHILDREN, AND DISPLAY OF DEAD BODIES 21:1-23

> **21** "If in the land which the Lord your God gives you to possess, any one is found slain, lying in the open country, and it is not known who killed him, [2]then your elders and your judges shall come forth, and they shall measure the distance to the cities which are around him that is slain; [3]and the elders of the city which is nearest to the slain man shall take a heifer which has never been worked and which has not pulled in the yoke. [4]And the elders of that city shall bring the heifer down to a valley with running water, which is neither plowed nor sown, and shall break the heifer's neck there in the valley. [5]And the priests the sons of Levi shall come forward,

for the Lord your God has chosen them to minister to him and to bless in the name of the Lord, and by their word every dispute and every assault shall be settled. ⁶And all the elders of that city nearest to the slain man shall wash their hands over the heifer whose neck was broken in the valley; ⁷and they shall testify, 'Our hands did not shed this blood, neither did our eyes see it shed. ⁸Forgive, O Lord, thy people Israel, whom thou hast redeemed, and set not the guilt of innocent blood in the midst of thy people Israel; but let the guilt of blood be forgiven them.' ⁹So you shall purge the guilt of innocent blood from your midst, when you do what is right in the sight of the Lord.

¹⁰"When you go forth to war against your enemies, and the Lord your God gives them into your hands, and you take them captive, ¹¹and see among the captives a beautiful woman, and you have desire for her and would take her for yourself as wife, ¹²then you shall bring her home to your house, and she shall shave her head and pare her nails. ¹³And she shall put off her captive's garb, and shall remain in your house and bewail her father and her mother a full month; after that you may go in to her, and be her husband, and she shall be your wife. ¹⁴Then, if you have no delight in her, you shall let her go where she will; but you shall not sell her for money, you shall not treat her as a slave, since you have humiliated her.''

Verses 1-8 envision the case of unsolved homicide. The ritual of the heifer is intended to avert pollution of the land, the ultimate aim of many of the laws. Forbidden acts like unauthorized killing destroys the sanctity of the Lord's land. The words of the ritual in vv. 7-8 imply the view that an unatoned sacrilegious act sets up a dangerous counter-force that can explode almost randomly upon the people of the vicinity. The elders, representing the people of the endangered vicinity, demonstrate concretely by the ritual of the slaughter and hand washing that they and their people are innocent. Their prayer is that "the guilt of innocent blood," i.e. the punishment due for the slaying of the innocent person, hang no longer over Israel (v. 8). People today unaccustomed to seeing the world replete with inherent laws or directions from primordial times find it difficult to understand the danger of sacrilege for the community. Such a world view was entirely compatible with belief in the Lord. The Levitical priests had to be on the scene (v. 5) to direct the elders in the proper exercise of the task of safeguarding their own locality. The fact that the heifer has never plowed, and the land has never been sown, shows the sacred character of the rite.

Verses 10-17 describe the case of the Israelite warrior desiring to marry a captive woman. In the light of 20:16-18, the woman would have to be from a "city very far from you," i.e. outside of the boundaries of Canaan. The case is that of a male, a warrior, as are many of the cases in Deuteronomy, yet the perspective is that of the woman. Respect for the woman's feelings—her need for time to mourn both her own captive state and the loss of her father and mother—is paramount, and takes precedence over the desire of the exuberant young warrior to enjoy immediately the fruits of his conquest.

At the risk of overgeneralization, one may say that the adult male normally plays the public role, whereas the adult female's role is in the domestic sphere. The domestic sphere is not without power, as is seen in the description of the upper class married woman in Prov 31:10-31. "She considers a field and buys it, with the fruit of her hands she plants a vineyard," and "She makes linen garments and sells them; she delivers girdles to the merchants." Women occasionally, though not normally, assumed public roles, as was the case with Deborah, Judith and others. Though the normal case of law envisions the adult male, the male represents the family among whom was the woman. This conception of public role differs to be sure from that in modern American society, but the woman's general absence from the legal cases proposed in Deuteronomy is not to be taken as it might be in American society, as a deliberate exclusion. It is rather simply the ancient mode of conceptualization of public and private roles. The man represents his household, unmarried siblings, wife, children, and slaves.

The woman's sensitivities determine the time and the mode of her captivity. First she is allowed to cut her hair and nails and put off the garb in which she was captured and to mourn for her many losses in accord with her custom. Then she may become the warrior's wife; the situation of polygamy is presupposed here as it is in vv. 15-17, since the warrior already has established his household, his "house" of v. 12. If the man is not pleased with his new bride, he may send her away to wherever *she* desires to go. He may not sell her.

The next law also concerns family life, and shows similar humanity toward potential victims—this time the son of the less favored wife. Polygamy is presupposed. The objective right of the first born is upheld. Hebrew law regularly assigned a double portion to the first born son, and this law is not to be tampered with by the machinations of favored wives in harem intrigues. The inalienable right of the first born, apart from any question of human merit, is clearly illustrated in the story of the patriarch Jacob and his brother Esau in Genesis 25-35. In the land, the law will assure that the less favored will receive their due.

Verses 18-21 foresee the case of the rebellious son who is to be stoned to death. The severity of the punishment reflects the respect the family enjoyed in Israel. A patriarchal society is built upon respect for "the elders," immediately the father and mother. "Honor your father and mother, as the Lord commanded you," in the Decalogue (5:16) showed already the place of parents and consequently the malice of continued and obstinate refusal to obey. Obviously the law is concerned with serious breaches of public order and not with the minor domestic squabbles that are part of children's growing up. The phrase "glutton and drunkard" is found in Prov 23:21 and 28:7; it is a

word pair like "stubborn and rebellious" that character-
izes the contemptuous and dissolute character of the child.
As in a number of other laws, the phrase "you shall purge
the evil from your midst" refers to the purifying of the holy people from the consequences of behavior so wicked
that reactive forces might explode over the whole people
unless the guilty party be located and purged. The salutary
lesson from just punishment swiftly executed is also a fac-
tor here.

The lesson from punishment is part of the last section of
the chapter—a body is not to be left on public display over-
night (vv. 22-23). Hanging was not the means of death.
After a person who was guilty of a capital offense had been
executed, the body would be displayed on a tree or wooden
post as a lesson to others, but only for a limited time. The
body of the criminal, being an accursed object because of
the sin, was to be buried before nightfall. The law limits
the display of accursed objects, with the aim of preserving
the sanctity of the land.

LAWS ON ASSISTANCE TO THE NEIGHBOR, ABOMINATIONS, AND INJUSTICE IN SEXUAL MATTERS
22:1-30

22 "You shall not see your brother's ox or his sheep go
astray, and withhold your help from them; you shall
take them back to your brother.

⁵"A woman shall not wear anything that pertains to a
man, nor shall a man put on a woman's garment; for
whoever does these things is an abomination to the Lord
your God.

⁹"You shall not sow your vineyard with two kinds of
seed, lest the whole yield be forfeited to the sanctuary,
the crop which you have sown and the yield of the
vineyard. ¹⁰You shall not plow with an ox and an ass
together. ¹¹You shall not wear a mingled stuff, wool and
linen together.

[13]"If any man takes a wife, and goes in to her, and then spurns her, [14]and charges her with shameful conduct, and brings an evil name upon her, saying, 'I took this woman, and when I came near her, I did not find in her the tokens of virginity,' [15]then the father of the young woman and her mother shall take and bring out the tokens of her virginity to the elders of the city in the gate; [16]and the father of the young woman shall say to the elders, 'I gave my daughter to this man to wife, and he spurns her; [17]and lo, he has made shameful charges against her, saying, "I did not find in your daughter the tokens of virginity." And yet these are the tokens of my daughter's virginity.' And they shall spread the garment before the elders of the city. [18]Then the elders of that city shall take the man and whip him; [19]and they shall fine him a hundred shekels of silver, and give them to the father of the young woman, because he has brought an evil name upon a virgin of Israel; and she shall be his wife; he may not put her away all his days. [20]But if the thing is true, that the tokens of virginity were not found in the young woman, [21]then they shall bring out the young woman to the door of her father's house, and the men of her city shall stone her to death with stones, because she has wrought folly in Israel by playing the harlot in her father's house; so you shall purge the evil from the midst of you.

[22]"If a man is found lying with the wife of another man, both of them shall die, the man who lay with the woman, and the woman; so you shall purge the evil from Israel."

Chapter 22 contains a variety of laws, only a few of which are related thematically, the prohibitions against mixing certain specifically different items, vv. 5, 9-11, and injustice in sexual behavior, vv. 13-30. Other laws, like the unique one of freeing the mother bird, are interspersed. As in the rest of chaps. 21-25, a good deal of disparate legal material has been gathered here.

Like many of the laws in Deuteronomy 12-25, the laws in this chapter appear also in other codes within the Bible. For example, the rule of returning lost animals is found in Exod 23:4-5 and the prohibition of non-natural combinations, in Lev 19:19. The genius of Deuteronomy is to have taken the old laws and set them in a new context of behavior in the good land which the Lord, the God of Israel, is giving them. The land is conceived as "the land on which you shall live." It is therefore the sphere of life graciously given by the Lord. Only this conception of the land where Israel "lives," i.e., exists near the Lord on the land, explains satisfactorily such phrases as, "that it may go well with you and that you may live long" (v. 7). This is the motive for letting the mother bird go free after one accidentally comes upon a bird's nest! The lawgiver is convinced that life in the land is graciously given and as a given must be directed in all its particulars by the *torah*. In one sense there is no distinction between great and slight laws. All are directed to guiding the Israelite to life in the land.

The random assortment of material in these chapters should surprise only those readers who expect the logical arrangement of a modern law code. Ancient codes were not so organized. Sometimes the individual laws were topically set out. More often they were not, being related sometimes by catchwords, purely mnemonic devices such as similar sounding words. Sometimes, as here, one finds clusters of related laws alongside of individual laws. Ancient law codes were not complete systems like the Napoleonic Code, or the Roman Catholic Code of Canon Law, but a promulgation of legal practice that was not taken to be exhaustive.

Verses 1-4 are concerned with the restoration of lost animals and the assistance of animals who have fallen from a shifting of their load. The version of the same law in another code can be instructively compared to see the Deuteronomic distinctiveness. In Exod 23:4-5, it reads: "If you meet your enemy's ox or his ass going astray, you shall bring it back to him. If you see the ass of one who hates you lying under its burdens, you shall refrain from leaving him with it, you shall help him to lift it up." One can see important emphases in Deuteronomy not present in Exodus. Deuteronomy envisions a single people inhabiting the land. The word "brother" does not refer exclusively to immediate family but can include all kin. So one is to think of one's neighbor as kin and as a fellow member of the Lord's people. The neighbor's ownership of his animals does not cease because they have become lost. The relationship between neighbors in Israel is too close for the cold impersonality of "finders-keepers" to prevail. If the owner is not known, or so distant that a journey would be too burdensome, the owner is to hold the animal until the true owner claims it (v. 2, *RSV* "seeks it"). The law is so concerned with upholding the fraternal duty of returning lost goods that it leaves untreated in vv. 2-3 the important question of appropriate payment due the finder for the expense of feeding the animal until its return. One can see here that the terse legal style of the old codes like the Covenant Code (Exod 20:22-23:33) has been adapted to the purposes of religious oratory. Exod 23:4-5 focused exclusively on animals, the case of oxen and asses, but Deut 22:3 extends the list of returnables to clothing and indeed to any item whatsoever. And the motive is clearer here than in the Covenant Code—the neighbor is one's "brother" (or sister, the Hebrew term includes male and female in this usage). The people are related and together are the recipients of the abundance of the Lord's gifts.

Verse 5 prohibits women wearing anything that pertains to a man—clothing, but also weapons and ornaments. Does the law have in mind transvestism as a sexual practice and by implication homosexuality, or does it refer to worship of deities in which the priest put on the garb of the deity—woman's for a goddess and man's for a god? This cultic practice is attested only in hellenistic times. We do not know. Homosexual behavior is forbidden in Lev 18:22. Below we shall see a law that prohibits mingling different species, and it may be that here the same taboo appears against mingling male and female in order to respect the distinctions inherent in the world (see under 22:6-9). The phrase "whoever does those things is an abomination to the Lord your God," can refer in Deuteronomy to cultic irregularity or simply to any reprehensible practice (as in 24:4).

Almost quaint to modern legal sensibility is the sparing of the mother in an inadvertent find of a bird's nest, a law unique to Deuteronomy. It is difficult to see how this is an instance of "Deuteronomic humanism," since the little birds are taken away for food. Rather, like 20:19-20 which protected fruit trees of the land in times of war, this is an ecological measure to protect the mother for future bearing. It is another sign of regard for the fertility of the land.

Unique also is the excerpt from a "building code." Ancient roofs were flat and were much used, for sleeping, for entertaining. The aim of the law reminds us how different can be the thought world of the ancients—"that you may not bring the guilt of blood upon your house, if any one fall from it." Persons can by their extreme carelessness make themselves liable to vengeance by the avenger of blood *(gō'ēl)*. To forestall occasions for private vengeance, one ought to take precautions, e.g., the building of a parapet or the filling in of an open pit (Exod 21:33-36).

The exact import of the prohibitions against mixing different kinds of things is not clear. Perhaps one meets again that respect for the inherent orders or gradations in the world which has been encountered already in 22:5. The thought of Gen 1:11 may be relevant. "And God said, 'Let the earth put forth vegetation, plants yielding seed, and fruit trees bearing fruit in which is their seed, each according to its kind, upon the earth" (cf. also Gen 1:12; 21, 24, 25). It is prohibited to sow between the vines. The whole crop, the grapes and the seed crop would be consecrated and not available for profane use were they to be mixed. Other "crossings of boundaries" are forbidden—plowing with an ox and an ass together and the combining of wool and linen in one garment. Jewish traditions

picked up and greatly expanded the traditions of prohibited pairs, in the Mishnaic tractate *Kil'aim,* "Pairs,"
the same Hebrew word which appears in v. 9.

Another prescription which passed into later Jewish law
is found in v. 12, regarding the tassels to be placed on the
four corners of the garment. In Num 15:37-41 the same injunction is given, to remind the wearer to do all the commandments and be holy to the Lord who brought them out
of Egypt. The mention of the law here may be triggered by
the garment mentioned in v. 11. In accord with this law,
Jews gradually began to place a tassel at each corner of the
large quadrangular garment commonly worn round the
body. In a still later age when the Jews were exiled from
Palestine and subject to persecution, the tassels were
transferred to the inner garment to avoid attention. Eventually the custom arose of attaching them to the *tallith,* or
quadrangular mantel, worn at the time of prayer.

The last part of the chapter is given entirely to a single
theme—sexual misconduct in the form of cases, "if a person . . . " Casuistic law is found elsewhere in the Bible
and is common in Mesopotamian law codes. The first case
is given in detail and the others are brief. The care for marriage evidenced here is another instance of the familial
basis of Israel's society, and its conservatism. The strict
marital morality does not arise from a view that sexuality is
evil and must be strictly limited or foresworn—such a basis
for asceticism is unknown in the Bible—but from the
perceived connection between private morality and public
order.

The case in vv. 13-21 is primarily that of a man who uses
the accusation that his bride was not a virgin to get out of
his marriage with her. The surprising judgment at the end
of v. 19 that the woman is to be the wife forever of the man
who had tried to destroy her and her family's reputation
makes sense in a legal context. The man has to support her
as a member of his household even if there were no more
personal relationship between the pair. The *RSV* of v. 14a,
"and charges her with shameful conduct," is a tentative

translation of a difficult verse. The sense is that the man makes up the charges out of thin air. The whole scene of husband's and parents' statements takes place "in the gate," the open space before the town gate where the local court sat. The young woman would probably be in her mid-teens and so unskilled in defending herself competently against the charges. The tokens of virginity which the parents present to the elders in the gate are the bloodied bedclothes. The blood is the sign of the girl's virginity and of the truth of the parents' statement over against the husband's. The evidence for the virginity is extremely concrete—the bloodied bedclothes. Virginity was often identified with its physical token.

Modern sensitivity may be offended by the subordinate role of women in this and the following laws in the chapter. The law does not treat her as it does the man. Her virginity seems at times to be a value separate from her person. The virginity of only the women is insisted upon prior to marriage. Such objections against the Bible are to be taken seriously as arising from a reverent desire to make the Bible relevant to modern views of women's right and dignity. In response, this and other laws regarding marriage came out of a society different from our own, a society which is not a model for us in all its particulars, e.g., its practice of slavery or its practice of sabbatical rest for the land. Sometimes the Bible does not prescribe. It simply describes, and we can be thankful for its non-idealizing honesty in recording the bad as well as the good. That point having been made, some understanding of the society of the time will help us see woman's place was not so bad as a first reading might suggest. First the male had the public and legal role, e.g., the husband and the father speak in the gate. The question here is a legal one—whether the woman was, as the man had a legal right to expect her to be, physically a virgin. The woman became part of the man's household; the man represents his household to the community. Granted the priority of the man in the public forum, mutuality is to characterize the relationship within the household. Honor and shame played a much more important role than in our society. A man would be shamed if he were duped in the expectation of his wife's virginity common at that time. Boys and girls were raised separately. There was no period of dating as allowed in modern societies. The parents customarily played a large role in the marriage of their young children. It would be expected that the girl's parents would have seen to her proper upbringing and protection. Lastly, the aim of several laws is to protect the woman.

Verses 20-22 considers the possibility that the husband's charges were true that the woman was not a virgin. She is to be stoned like the foolish and rebellious son in 21:21. She has "wrought folly in Israel," a phrase nearly always of sexual misconduct. She has disgraced her father's house. The evil must be purged by death.

The case of adultery in v. 22 considers the woman to be part of the household of the man. The husband's rights have been violated. The man's marital status is not mentioned since it is irrelevant to this legal question.

The next cases in vv. 23-27 envision an engaged woman who is treated as if she were already married. The bride-price has already been paid for her and she is considered part of her husband's household. An assumption is made for judging the possible complicity of the woman in cases of rape—the woman would naturally cry out and be heard in a city. In the country it would be assumed that no one would hear her and come to the rescue.

In v. 28, a couple caught in fornication—the woman is neither married nor engaged—is assumed to be on the way to marriage. At any rate the woman is protected. The Israelites thought in their laws of sexual intercourse as a step to marriage. Sexual intercourse was excluded from the Israelite worship system, though it seems to have played a role in Canaanite cult. It is here located in the context of permanent union between man and wife in a legally fixed household.

The last law, in v. 30, states one of the forbidden degrees

of kinship for marriage, the stepmother. One of the Hebrew idioms for taking a wife, which originated in a symbolic legal act, was "to spread the skirt over [the woman]," as in Ezek 16:8 and Ruth 3:9. The man signified publicly that he would take the woman into his household by symbolically clothing her. Hence for the son "to remove his father's garment"—so reads the Hebrew literally in place of the confusing *RSV*—means that the son takes over from his father the husband's role. That is forbidden.

LAWS CONCERNING THE ASSEMBLY, AND OTHER MATTERS
23:1-25

23 "He whose testicles are crushed or whose male member is cut off shall not enter the assembly of the Lord.

²"No bastard shall enter the assembly of the lord; even to the tenth generation none of his descendants shall enter the assembly of the Lord.

³"No Ammonite or Moabite shall enter the assembly of the Lord; even to the tenth generation none belonging to them shall enter the assembly of the Lord for ever; ⁴because they did not meet you with bread and with water on the way, when you came forth out of Egypt, and because they hired against you Balaam the son of Be'or from Pethor of Mesoptamia, to curse you. ⁵Nevertheless the Lord your God would not hearken to Balaam; but the Lord your God turned the curse into a blessing for you, because the Lord your God loved you. ⁶You shall not seek their peace or their prosperity all your days for ever.

⁷"You shall not abhor an Edomite, for he is your brother; you shall not abhor an Egyptian, because you were a sojourner in his land. ⁸The children of the third generation that are born to them may enter the assembly of the Lord."

Chapter 23 contains miscellaneous laws, arranged according to two topic sentences, "you shall (not) . . ." or "when you do such and such. . . ." Verses 1-14 are concerned with a broadly similar theme, conditions for membership in the holy community. The rest of the laws on the reception of runaway slaves, cult prostitution, lending at interest, vows, and casual eating in a neighbor's field, are united only by the extrinsic introductory devices just mentioned.

The two introductions, "you shall (not). . . ," and "when you do such and such. . . ," pertain to the two basic types of ancient Near Eastern law, casuistic and apodictic. Of the two, casuistic law was by far the more common throughout the East, being found in the law codes. Apodictic law is almost exclusively a biblical phenomenon; it expresses the firm roots of law in the divine will. It thus fits into the suzerain-vassal covenant where behavior of each part is rooted in an affective relationship.

Verses 1-8 regulate the membership of the assembly of the Lord. The term "assembly of the Lord" does not embrace all who lived within the Israelite community, e.g. resident aliens, non-Hebrew slaves, foreign mercenaries and the like, but only the covenanted people particularly when gathered for worship. The normal context of the noun "assembly" in Deuteronomy is Horeb/Sinai (4:10; 5:22; 9:10; 10:4 and 18:16) because that is the crystallizing moment of Israel's relation to the Lord. There "before the Lord" through the mediation of Moses, Israel became the people of the Lord and the Lord became their God. Admittance to this sacral community is divinely regulated. No one admits himself or herself. Hence these rules. The Hebrew word for "assembly," *qāhāl,* is translated in the Septuagint by *ekklēsia,* a word which the New Testament uses to designate "congregation" or "church."

The way by which the sacred community is defined in vv. 1-6 is by the kinds of people excluded. Contemporary religious societies are apt to define themselves differently, and stress the interior attitude proper for membership. But these verses do not presuppose a modern voluntary association but rather a group already defined by blood. Its focus is on disqualifying external marks.

The first group excluded is eunuchs, made so by surgical operation. Eunuchs in Eastern courts often rose to prominence. The Bible attests their high place in the Israelite royal administration, e.g. 1 Sam 8:15; 1 Kings 22:9; 2 Kings 8:6, etc. *RSV* often translates the Hebrew term *sārîs,* used in the above passages, by "officer." An oriental court would ordinarily have a harem supervised by eunuchs. The law here takes the same attitude toward physical integrity that it does in its insistence on only unblemished animals as firstlings (15:21). More may be meant by the exclusion if, as some authors think, men became eunuchs in order to take part in foreign rites. Evidence from hellenistic times attests frenzied self-mutilation in honor of various goddesses. Those permanently marked by their devotion to "other gods" could never take part in the worship of the one Lord.

The prohibition against bastards in v. 2 may likewise be more limited than first appears. Offspring of incestuous union, i.e., within the forbidden degrees of marriage, might be here intended. So later rabbinic tradition.

Two national groups are excluded "to the tenth generation," i.e. forever, because of what their ancestors did to the Israelites in their march through Transjordan. Enmity between Israel and its Transjordanian neighbors was a constant in Israel's foreign relations. These tensions are interpreted as arising from the time of the exodus-conquest, as in Deuteronomy 2; Numbers 21-24, or even from primordial times, as in Gen 19:30-38. The true nature of the people was thought to have been expressed once and for all in their early conduct. Despite the Moabites' attempt to curse Israel using the seer, Baalam, the curse turned into a blessing. Israel remained forever blessed by God and the Moabites forever outside the blessing (vv. 4-5). Israel is never to make a treaty with them—so the meaning of v. 6. The words for "peace and prosperity" are words for "treaty," as recent research has demonstrated.

The possibility of good relationships with another Transjordanian neighbor, the Edomites, is left open, and also with Egypt, despite the bondage endured in the latter country (v. 7). The reasons for friendship are given, as they were given for enmity above. Edom is kin, the kinship being evidently based on descent from Esau, the brother of the ancestor Jacob-Israel. Israel was a resident alien in Egypt. Egyptian (and Edomite) resident aliens of the third generation may join the Israelite community.

Verses 9-14 concern Israel's conduct on campaign. The warriors in a holy war were dedicated to the Lord who was seen as present within the camp as he guided his troops. These rules resemble liturgical norms since they regulate conduct near the Lord. Like them, they are not concerned with motives, but only with external actions, determining whether they are appropriate or inappropriate. "Keep yourself from any evil thing" in v. 9, means from anything untoward. Sexual activity, even inadvertent nocturnal discharge of semen is an untoward action and must be compensated for. When David was on campaign, he explained concerning his soldiers, "Of a truth women have been kept from us as always when I go on an expedition: the vessels of the young men are holy, even when it is a common journey; how much more today will their vessels be holy?" (1 Sam 21:5). Anything shameful is to be avoided because the Lord walks through the camp. Dignity, so important to an Israelite, was bound up with his external appearances, his beard and clothes. Dignity and hygiene led the Israelite warrior to perform his toilet outside the camp.

Verses 15-16 concern foreign slaves who escape to Israel and ask for asylum. They are not to be returned to their masters. The slave is free to choose his place of settlement. No motive is given for the policy. It is worth recalling that frequently in ancient sovereignty treaties there are provisions for the vassal to return runaways from the suzerain's state. Israel, free of suzerain treaties except with the Lord, need not return slaves. The custom is in keeping with its national story of slavery to freedom.

The next laws prohibit cultic prostitution and the use of tainted money in Israelite worship (vv. 17-18). To understand cultic prostitution one must keep in mind the near obsession of ancient peoples with fertility—in themselves, their animals, their land. Refrigeration did not exist, nor did canning, nor most of the effective means used in modern times to preserve food for periods of drought and blight. Ancient farmers sought every means of enhancing seasonal fertility with the goal of preserving their own life and that of their households. One means was to engage in exemplary acts of sex in the temple area with the hope that these would help along the process of fertility in all aspects of life. For a man or woman the most intense expression of fertility was the act of intercourse. The above reflections on cultic prostitution are conjectural. The ancients have not left us reasoned accounts of their rituals.

Such manipulation of fertility by cultic prostitutes is out of the question for Israel. The money gained in such idolatrous transactions is not to be used for any purpose in the house of the Lord. "Dog" is the Hebrew word for male cult prostitute, though the word may not have had that pejorative meaning in other languages. The word for cult prostitute, male or female, in Hebrew is from the root "holy." "Holy," of course, does not primarily have the modern meaning of moral probity but of proximity to the divine sphere. Anyone who exercises a cultic function is "holy" in this sense.

The next law, the prohibition of lending at interest in vv. 19-20, has already been discussed under 15:1-11. In ancient times, commercial ventures requiring borrowed capital were unknown, and loans were almost exclusively for the relief of distress. To demand interest among "brothers" would be to profit from the distress of another. The condemnation of the practice of taking interest on money lent is also found among Greek and Roman thinkers. As a motive the prospect of divine blessing in the land is held out. There is also a hint, if not an assurance, that the Lord will endow those who obey with wealth so that they will never need to supplement their income by taking interest.

Caution both in making vows in the first place and about filling them speedily afterwards, is the theme of vv. 21-23. Some of the Wisdom literature, Proverbs and Qoheleth specifically, have the same cautious attitude toward vows and their fulfillment. One can see behind the advice a belief about the dignity and adult responsibility for everything said "before the Lord." What is promised in that context is taken with the utmost seriousness not only because of the majesty of the Lord who hears, but also because of the immense dignity of the one who promises.

The law of picking grain or grapes while walking through a field (vv. 24-25) shows up in a New Testament controversy (Mark 2:23, Matt 12:1, Luke 6:1). Jesus takes the same sensible and humane attitude as does the original law. The criterion is wise. One may pick and eat, but may not use a basket which would indicate that hospitality is being abused and theft committed. The same principle is even clearer with regard to standing grain where one may not use a sickle that would cut it in quantity. The law breathes a generous and hospitable spirit for all its practicality, a spirit of life gratefully lived among "brothers" and "sisters" in the land the Lord gives. Deut 24:19-22 shows the same attitude.

Chapter 23 combines a sense of the transcendence of the Lord and the distinctiveness of his chosen people in the land of promise.

LAWS CONCERNING MARRIAGE AND PROTECTION OF THE DEFENSELESS
24:1-22

24 "When a man takes a wife and marries her, if then she finds no favor in his eyes because he has found some indecency in her, and he writes her a bill of divorce and puts it in her hand and sends her out of his house, and she departs out of his house, ²and if she goes and

becomes another man's wife, ³and the latter husband
dislikes her and writes her a bill of divorce and puts it in
her hand and sends her out of his house, or if the latter
husband dies, who took her to be his wife, ⁴then her
former husband, who sent her away, may not take her
again to be his wife, after she has been defiled; for that
is an abomination before the Lord, and you shall not
bring guilt upon the land which the Lord your God gives
you for an inheritance.

¹⁰"When you make your neighbor a loan of any sort,
you shall not go into his house to fetch his pledge. ¹¹You
shall stand outside, and the man to whom you make the
loan shall bring the pledge out to you. ¹²And if he is a
poor man, you shall not sleep in his pledge; ¹³when the
sun goes down, you shall restore to him the pledge that
he may sleep in his cloak and bless you; and it shall be
righteousness to you before the Lord your God.

¹⁴"You shall not oppress a hired servant who is poor
and needy, whether he is one of your brethren or one of
the sojourners who are in your land within your towns;
¹⁵you shall give him his hire on the day he earns it,
before the sun goes down (for he is poor, and sets his
heart upon it); lest he cry against you to the Lord, and it
be sin in you."

The contents of chap. 24 are more clearly related to each
other than was true of previous chapters. Verses 1-5 concern marriage, and the remainder, with the exception of
vv. 8-9 on leprosy, has to do with the protection of
defenseless groups in society.

Verses 1-4 is so tersely laid out that its full import is not
clear today. The first three verses state the conditions, and
the last verse, v. 4, gives the decision. The right of divorce
is assumed. The husband gives the wife a bill of divorce
because he has found in her *'erwat dābār,* lit. "nakedness
of a thing," an uncertain Hebrew phrase that is translated
differently in different translations, "some indecency" in
RSV and "something obnoxious" in the *New Jewish Ver-*

sion. It surely is not adultery, since that would incur the death penalty. The term may simply be a general one for an objective fault in the wife that justifies legal divorce. The wife marries again and then, either through a second divorce or through the death of her second husband, becomes free. The first husband may not take her to wife again for she has been "defiled," i.e. disqualified for him. The grounds for the "defilement" are not explained. In any case remarriage would be an abomination before the Lord, and would bring "defilement" (the same word used of the woman) upon the land.

The second law regarding marriage exempts the newly married man from military service and other business (probably imposed state labor, from the context) for the period of one year. Exemption for newlyweds has been mentioned in 20:7 on slightly different grounds, to supply the army with combat ready troops.

The rest of the chapter, with the exception of vv. 8-9, centers on protection for the needy. Verse 6 prohibits taking in pledge of loan repayment the hand-mill, i.e., either the two flat circular stones worked usually by two women seated on the ground, or the upper millstone which would of course render the whole mill unusable. To take such basic tools of daily life would be equivalent to taking a life in pledge. The law restricts untrammeled freedom of creditors and bars them from intruding into private acts. Loans were generally made to those in need and the debtor would be in straitened circumstances already without having to undergo further indignities.

Kidnapping is probably intended by the seventh commandment, "Neither shall you steal" (5:19 and Exod 20:15). The victim would typically be poor, the kind of person unprotected by social position or by a family that could offer the protection of an energetic avenger. Kidnapping was not for ransom as generally today, but to enslave the unfortunate victim or to sell the person into a foreign land. The perpetrator is to die that the evil be purged from the land. No one has the right to take the Israelite from his divinely given land.

Verses 8-9 are not so much concerned with leprosy as they are with obeying the priests. In Leviticus 13 and 14 the Priestly Code prescribes for leprosy and includes a wealth of detail that only professional priests could be expected to master. Leprosy in the Bible covered a wider variety of infectious skin disorders than the modern medical definition of leprosy. The priests in diagnosing and treating the disease acted like public health officers, checking for sores, determining from their lore when the affected person could return to society. The priest is to be obeyed scrupulously since public order is at stake. Here again hygiene and holiness are closely related. The example of Miriam is adduced (Num 12:10-15) who was not cured until the time determined by divine decree had elapsed.

The same control over intrusive creditors, as in the prohibition against taking a millstone in pledge (v. 6), is seen again in vv. 10-12. The person is allowed to be master of his house; the creditor is to stand outside and wait at the door. A common pledge was the garment, a blanket-like piece of clothing used as a cloak by day and a bed-covering by night. It was to be returned at sundown to the poor person to sleep in, lest the poor wretch spend the night shivering in his undergarments. That the law was truly needed is shown by the prophet Amos in 760 B.C. who accuses wrongdoers, "they lay themselves down beside every altar upon garments taken in pledge" (Amos 2:8). A letter from a poor laborer to the commander complaining about his mistreatment at the hands of a subordinate officer brings the law vividly to life. The letter was written about 625 B.C., and published only in 1960. "May my lord, the commander, hear the word of his servant. As for your servant, your servant was harvesting in Hasir Asam; and your servant harvested, took measure, and arranged its storage according to custom before the sabbath. When your servant had measured the harvest and stored it up according to custom, Hawshyahu, son of Shobay, came and took the garment of your servant. When I had harvested this harvest of mine according to custom, he took the garment of your servant. And all of my brothers can testify for me, those who were with me in the heat of the sun. My brothers can testify for me! Truly, I am innocent of guilt. Return, please, the garment of mine. And if it is not for the commander to return the garment of your servant, show mercy to your servant and do not drive him away." For the creditor to obey the law brought righteousness, the right relationship of the obedient person to the Lord.

Verses 14-15, on the necessity of treating hired hands well and not delaying their payment, continue the same emphasis on social justice. Poor people cannot wait for pay at the master's convenience; money is always short and it should be paid on the day of work. The poor have only one source of strength and it is a powerful one—the Lord!

The next law was real in a society where a man's household was thought to be such a part of his person that it could suffer punishment for his sins. At least for capital offenses, only the actually guilty party is to die. It is a freeing concept, as is the text in Ezekiel 18 which it resembles.

In vv. 17-18 one meets three groups which appear like stereotypes in Hebrew rhetoric, indeed in the literature of other nations as well. The groups have none to defend them and stand in special need of the king's protection. They are the resident alien (*RSV* "sojourner"), the fatherless, and the widows. Ancient Eastern kings boasted that they cared for the neglected of society with fatherly care. The context in this law, however, is distinctively Israelite though the vocabulary is not new. All Israelites, not just the king, are responsible for the poor on the assumption that Israel is to be steeped in the memory of its oppression by Pharaoh and will instinctively aid any defenseless person.

Prosperous farmers are addressed in vv. 19-22. They are not to be so efficient in harvesting fields, beating down olive trees, and picking grapes that nothing at all is left to the poor who pick over the fields after the main harvesting. As the Book of Ruth portrays so touchingly in chap. 2, compassionate farmers would deliberately leave something in the field for the poor to gather. Two motives are mentioned for the practice: the Lord will bless the farmer for his "studied carelessness," making up for the lost produce; the memory of once being a slave in Egypt will aid Israel in remembering that the land is not theirs by right but by grace. Its yield is a gift and gifts are best shared.

LAWS REGULATING CORPORAL PUNISHMENT, LEVIRATE MARRIAGE, JUST WEIGHTS, AND OTHER MATTERS
25:1-19

25 "If there is a dispute between men, and they come into court, and the judges decide between them, acquitting the innocent and condemning the guilty, ²then if the guilty man deserves to be beaten, the judge shall cause him to lie down and be beaten in his presence with a number of stripes in proportion to his offense. ³Forty stripes may be given him, but not more; lest, if one should go on to beat him with more stripes than these, your brother be degraded in your sight.

⁴"You shall not muzzle an ox when it treads out the grain.

¹⁷"Remember what Amalek did to you on the way as you came out of Egypt, ¹⁸how he attacked you on the way, when you were faint and weary, and cut off at your rear all who lagged behind you; and he did not fear God. ¹⁹Therefore when the Lord your God has given you rest from all your enemies round about, in the land which the Lord your God gives you for an inheritance to possess, you shall blot out the remembrance of Amalek from under heaven; you shall not forget.

With chap. 25 the specific laws of the Code come to an end. Chapters 26-28 contain actions to be performed upon entry, liturgical conclusions, some according to the pattern of the covenant formulary with its expected curses and

blessings. The mention of the Amalekites in vv. 17-19 may
be intended to round out the section beginning in 23:1
which also urges hostility against a historical enemy, the
Edomites. In addition, the mention of the "rest of your
enemies round about" in v. 19 possibly directs attention to
the beginning of the specific laws in chap. 12, where the
same phrase occurs, "you have not yet come to the rest
and inheritance which the Lord your God gives you."

As in other chapters within the section of chaps. 12-25,
the laws are not arranged sytematically but rather offer a
sample of the new spirit of observance.

The first two laws are peculiar to Deuteronomy. One
regulates the severity of corporal punishment, and the
other looks after working animals. The case in vv. 1-3 is
that of an individual who is found guilty of a crime that requires a penalty of corporal punishment rather than, say,
of simple restitution of property. A proper finding of guilt
is assumed. The law regulates the punishment. The whip-
ping is to take place in the presence of the judge so that it be
no more or less severe than the judge has determined. Forty stripes is the upper limit beyond which human honor
was irreparably demeaned. Later Jewish tradition limited
the stripes to thirty-nine to avoid the possibility of going
over. Preserving the dignity of even a convicted criminal is
an important value to be upheld by the practical expedient
of requiring the presence of the presiding judge and fixing
a limit to the number of strokes.

The next law, v. 4, that oxen treading grain are not to be
muzzled, reflects the sensitive and generous spirit that will
characterize Israelite enjoyment of their land. The oxen,
yoked in pairs, are led around the threshing floor,
separating the grain from the husk by the pressure of their
sharp hooves. To prevent laboring oxen from occasionally
eating the grain that surrounds them is cruel in the
Deuteronomic perspective. St. Paul in 1 Cor 9:9 and 1 Tim
5:18 quotes the law in support of the principle that laborers
for the gospel are worthy of their hire.

The next law regulates the levirate marriage and was

designed to prevent alienation of property. The deceased husband's brother was to raise up a son to inherit the property of the dead man. The assumption here is that inheritance of land was through the son, though Num 27:8 gives the right to daughters. "Levirate" comes from the Latin *levir,* "husband's brother."

The legal conditions for the levirate duty are quite specific: adjoining property of the two brothers, no male issue to the dead brother, and the cessation of the obligation with the birth of a son. Given the delicate nature of the duty, the law recognizes it cannot be forced and operates on the level of public honor and shame to achieve its practice. The woman is legally provided a means of shaming a hesitant surviving brother. She may bring the matter to the attention of the whole village through their representatives, the elders. She could declare the refusal publically and set in motion a legal process. The brother must declare his refusal to do his levirate duty before the elders of the village. If he persists, the wife pulled off his sandal and split in his face and cursed him, "So shall it be done to the man who does not build up his brother's house." Legal deeds were often accompanied by gestures which showed dramatically the reality of the legal exchange. When one sold a piece of property, for instance, one handed one's shoe to the buyer, showing that the right to walk on the property as its owner has been given up to the buyer. Here the surviving brother lets the land slip out of family control; this is equivalent to transfer of ownership. Hence the stripping off of the sandal. The law in Deuteronomic fashion is concerned with the land which the Lord gives, emphasizing how disgraceful it is not to pass the land on to legitimate descendants.

The law simply assumes that the practice of levirate marriage is one of the mechanisms by which the land is passed on to heirs, as in Genesis 38. It regulates that handing on especially when the poor, "the widow," might lose out.

A somewhat more violent scene is encountered in vv. 11-12, the punishment of the wife who assists her husband in a fight by grabbing the genitals of his opponent. It is the only place outside of the law of talion where physical mutilation is prescribed. Outside the Bible, mutilation was a common penalty.

False weights in commercial transactions are forbidden in vv. 13-16, a prohibition also found in Lev 19:35-36. Fixed coinage was not introduced until the Persian period in the sixth century. Before that time precious metals were weighed, as indeed were most commodities, using standardized weights. The danger of abuse was always great since the naked eye could not tell if a weight had been shaved for selling or augmented for buying. Dishonest activity in commerce offends the new order of behavior in the land. Honesty is the way to live more surely the life offered by the Lord. Dishonesty, perhaps because it is hard to detect and police by ordinary means, becomes an "abomination" that invites direct divine in intervention.

The last section on the Amalekites, vv. 17-19, as has been suggested, may round out the section beginning in 23:1, which also concerned those excluded from the Lord's community. The Amalekites were a desert tribe who claimed control of an area around Kadesh where Israel had encamped for many years, and from which it had tried to storm Canaan. An attack by the Amalekites is narrated in Exod 17:8-14. After Israel repulsed the attack, "the Lord said to Moses, "Write this as a memorial in a book [i.e. inscribe this in a document as a reminder] and recite it in the ears of Joshua, that I will utterly blot out the remembrance of Amalek from under heaven" (Exod 17:14). At the time of the writing of Deuteronomy, the Amalekites had long since ceased to exist as a tribe threatening Israel's existence. Their disappearance is here credited to the zeal of the generation of Israelites who carried out the written precept. The generation that wiped out the Amalekites in obedience to the written statute serves as an example to Israel of the need to defend itself from the nations around them. Such self-defense is the import of chap. 7 and particularly of chap. 12 which is alluded to here. Chapters

12-25 form a unified section. The insistance in the last law upon the annihilation of the historical enemy of Israel emphasizes that the laws aim to make Israel a distinctive people, separate from the nations.

LITURGICAL CEREMONIES FOR TITHING OF FIRST FRUITS. FROM LEGAL CODE TO TREATY. 26:1-19

26 "When you come into the land which the Lord your God gives for an inheritance, and have taken possession of it, and live in it, ²you shall take some of the first of all the fruit of the ground, which you harvest from your land that the Lord your God gives you, and you shall put it in a basket, and you shall go to the place which the Lord your God will choose, to make his name to dwell there.

⁵"And you shall make response before the Lord your God, 'A wandering Aramean was my father; and he went down into Egypt and sojourned there, few in number; and there he became a nation, great, mighty, and populous. ⁶And the Egyptians treated us harshly, and afflicted us, and laid upon us hard bondage. ⁷Then we cried to the Lord the God of our fathers, and the Lord heard our voice, and saw our affliction, our toil, and our oppression; ⁸and the Lord brought us out of Egypt with a mighty hand and an outstretched arm, with great terror, with signs and wonders; ⁹and he brought us into this place and gave us this land, a land flowing with milk and honey. ¹⁰And behold, now I bring the first of the fruit of the ground, which thou, O Lord, hast given me.'

¹⁶"This day the Lord your God commands you to do these statutes and ordinances; you shall therefore be careful to do them with all your heart and with all your soul. ¹⁷You have declared this day concerning the Lord

that he is your God, and that you will walk in his ways, and keep his statutes and his commandments and his ordinances, and will obey his voice; [18]and the Lord has declared this day concerning you that you are a people for his own possession, as he has promised you, and that you are to keep all his commandments, [19]that he will set you high above all nations that he has made, in praise and in fame and in honor, and that you shall be a people holy to the Lord your God, as he has spoken."

Chapter 26 contains instructions for liturgical ceremonies immediately upon entering the land. Its last verses, vv. 16-17, prepare directly for the conclusions of the covenant ceremony, the solemn blessings and curses of chaps. 27 and 28.

The first sections, vv. 1-11 and 12-15, are liturgical confessions, one for the first tithe in the new land and the other for the first triennial tithe. Both tithes have been dealt with before and in the same order in 14:22-29. Chapter 26 differs from that chapter in not being concerned with specifying the items to be tithed and their conversion into money when the items themselves cannot be brought to the central sanctuary. Chapter 26 is interested only in the first fruits of the soil, not with animal firstlings. The emphasis is on the confession of faith made by the Israelites in the central shrine. Here the modern reader needs to appreciate the importance for the Israelite of the first reported instance of a practice. This initial moment frequently displayed the full meaning of that event. For example, the first man and woman in the Garden illustrate with privileged clarity the situation of every man and woman. Abraham, the first believer in the Lord's promise, is the father of believers. By describing the first occurrence of tithing in the land, the text actually deals with the intent Israel should have in every act of tithing.

As Norbert Lohfink has pointed out, vv. 16-19 are of crucial importance because they turn legal lore into cove-

nant stipulations. Verse 17 piles up the traditional designations for laws, "his statutes and his commandments and
his ordinances," and situates them in the text of an ancient
Near Eastern treaty.

We turn to the details of the chapter. The first two verses
could not be more clear that the act of offering is to be the
spontaneous response to the Lord's gift of the land. Only
when Israel actually possesses the land are they able to
return it to the Lord through tithing. The Israelite is to put
the produce in a basket and bring it to the place which the
Lord chooses. Nothing is said about changing the produce
into money for ease of transportation to the central shrine
(cf., in contrast 14:25-26). It appears that at the first instance, produce is to be brought directly in a basket so that
the acknowledgment of the Lord's generous gift of the
land may stand out as clearly as possible. The juxtaposed
Deuteronomic phrases "the place which the Lord your
God will choose" and "to make his name dwell there" express the cultic presence of the Lord where the gifts are appropriately brought. The worshippers solemnly declare
before the priest in v. 3 that they have entered the land and
so identify themselves with their ancestors to whom God
first gave the land according to the confession of vv. 5-10a.
The priest's acceptance of the basket represents God's
good pleasure with the gift.

The confession of faith that the Israelite makes is a rich
summary of the whole national story—from the patriarchal beginnings, the increase of the people in Egypt leading
to their enslavement and eventually their liberation, the
leading through the wilderness to the land. As the Israelites
stand upon the land as its proprietors, the final goal of the
whole complex drama has been reached. The Israelites offer to the Lord a visible sign that the land is really God's
gift and loan to them. They are ready for grateful recital of
their faith. "Wandering" is the most likely translation of
an ambiguous Hebrew word, the adjective characterizing
the landless patriarchal generations ("your fathers"

elsewhere in Deuteronomy) who held the land only in promise. "Aramean" reflects the north Syrian origin of the whole line of patriarchs, the last of whom, Jacob, went down into Egypt. Egypt is the place where Israel became a numerous people, the patriarchal promise of numerous progeny coming true there just as the patriarchal promise of land becomes visible in this act of the initial tithing. Within the confession there is a dramatic contrast between Egypt with its hard bondage and Canaan with its miraculous abundance, "flowing with milk and honey." The Lord transferred his people from one realm to the other. Acknowledgment is to be made of this act. Verse 11 speaks of a feast which the Israelite is to enjoy at the time of the first tithe. Like the feast which is part of the regular tithing ceremony (14:26-27), this feast is to be shared with those outside the family group, in particular the Levite and the resident alien.

The very first triennial tithe also has its own particular confession in vv. 12-15. The regulations have been laid down in 14:28-29, that it is to be stored in kind within the towns for the poor. The Israelite is to affirm that he has removed, literally "purged," from his house "the holy portion." The holy portion is the tithed produce which as belonging to the Lord is not to be kept in a profane household. As holy it is to be disposed of according to ritual. The ritual here demands that the holy portion be given to the poor, "the Levite, the sojourner, the fatherless, and the widow." Verse 14 continues the confession in a negative way: eating of the tithe while mourning or otherwise unclean, or placing a portion of it with the corpse in a burial rite would have desecrated it. The Lord commands its "safe disposal" in only one way—free distribution to the poor. The idea seems to be that these classes of people who do not own a plot of land are nonetheless to enjoy its bounty. The confession ends in prayer that the blessing experienced on the day of enjoyment of first fruits continue in the future, further enhanc-

ing the life of the people and the life of their land according to the enduring promise to the patriarchs (v. 15).

As mentioned, vv. 16-19 transform the code into the text
of a treaty. "Today" (*RSV* "this day," as in 5:1, 3 and
elsewhere) situates the hearer in a liturgical assembly. The
exhortation to keep all the commandments with all one's
heart is what we expect to hear from the Mosaic officer.
The exact translation of v. 17 is not clear because the verb
form occurs only here. In crude literalness, it declares,
"you have caused the Lord to say," but the meaning is "to
let someone say" or "accept what someone says." Thus,
"you have agreed today to the declaration of the Lord *that*
he will be your God, *that* you will walk in his ways, *that*
you will keep his statutes, his commandments, and his ordinances, *that* you will obey his voice. The Lord has agreed
today to your declaration *that* you are ready to be his people, a special possession. . ." The Lord commits himself to
make the people his very own, and the people commit
themselves to obey him, but each makes a claim on the
other. Each declaration has four clauses (beginning with
"that" in my translation) of which only one expresses the
obligations assumed by the declaring party while the other
three state the partner's obligations. The Lord declares
that he will be Israel's God and demands with three different formulations that they serve him. Israel declares it
will obey the Lord's commandments with their three conditions: being made his special possession (Heb. *segulla,* as
in 7:6), being exalted above all nations, and being holy, i.e.
set apart. This is legal language of the treaty, albeit of parity rather than suzerainty-vassal treaty. The initiative of the
Lord is sufficiently clear throughout the whole book to
avoid any impression of simple equality between God and
Israel. The parity comes from the personal involvement of
the parties, the encounter of two free beings committing
themselves to each other. In v. 19 the three conditions
which Israel fulfills as the Lord's people are reduceable to
one—the people Israel as the favorite of the one powerful

Lord cannot but reflect on earth his priority and luster in the heavenly world.

Section 4.

LITURGICAL CEREMONY AT SHECHEM UPON ENTERING THE LAND.
27:1-26

27 Now Moses and the elders of Israel commanded the people, saying, "Keep all the commandment which I command you this day. ²And on the day you pass over the Jordan to the land which the Lord your God gives you, you shall set up large stones, and plaster them with plaster; ³and you shall write upon them all the words of this law, when you pass over to enter the land which the Lord your God gives you, a land flowing with milk and honey, as the Lord, the God of your fathers, has promised you.

⁹And Moses and the Levitical priests said to all Israel, "Keep silence and hear, O Israel: this day you have become the people of the Lord your God. ¹⁰You shall therefore obey the voice of the Lord your God, keeping his commandments and his statutes, which I command you this day."

²⁶"'Cursed be he who does not confirm the words of this law by doing them.' And all the people shall say, 'Amen.'

Chapter 27 is complex, being made up of several originally diverse parts, which now describe a single ceremony at Shechem. Mounts Ebal and Gerizim overlook this city with its ancient shrine. Blessings (v. 12) and curses are recited by the whole people under the leadership of Moses and the Levites. The event is to take place on the very day Israel crosses the Jordan (v. 2). This ceremony is more immediate than the liturgical ceremonies of tithing in chap. 26 which must wait upon a harvest. The ceremony of writing the law upon the stones with the action of blessing and cursing takes place on the very day the people enter the land. Israel is to encounter the words of the law from the very moment of its possession of the land.

The day is an important one in the Deuteronomist's eyes, who was preparing for it already in 12:26-32. The actual carrying out of these commands by Joshua is described in Josh 8:30-35. The unusual emphasis upon the law, from the twice repeated commands and from the explicit mention of fulfillment by Joshua, make clear how important it is that Israel consciously choose a life of obedience.

As stated above, chap. 27 is complex, made up of originally distinct elements. Investigating those units and their arrangement with a critical eye will teach us much about the chapter and its meaning. In v. 1, Moses is spoken of in the third person, interrupting Moses' direct speech of the preceding and subsequent chapters. The interruption and several inconsistencies within the chapter have led most scholars to suggest chap. 27 is an insertion into an already existing chaps. 5-28, made perhaps during the second edition of the Deuteronomistic History at the time of the exile. The chapter now situates the blessings and curses of chap. 28 in a ceremony on the very day of entry at Shechem. It suggests that the great covenant ceremony in Joshua 24 at Shechem with its stone of witness (Josh 24:26-27) continues the tradition begun here. The localizing of the ceremony at Shechem is surprising in view of the Deuteronomic description of the central shrine elsewhere. Even the reading of the law (31:11) is to be done at "the place which the Lord your God will choose." Apparently Shechem is the first of the central shrines.

Verses 1-3 speak of large steles or stone slabs upon which the law was to be inscribed. It was customary to engrave important decrees and laws upon slabs. In certain biblical passages, a large slab is set up as a witness to solemn agreements. Gen 31:52 reads, "And Laban said to

Jacob, . . . 'this mound shall be witness and this pillar shall be witness that I am not to cross to you past this mound. . . .' " In Josh 24:27, "Behold this stone shall be a witness against us; for it has heard all the words of the Lord which he spoke to us; therefore it shall be a witness against you, lest you deal falsely with your God." The stone "sees" whether Israel lives up to the law. Verse 4 says that the slabs are set up at Mt. Ebal, about eighteen miles in a direct line from the Jordan, an impossible distance for a whole people to journey on the day of their entry. It seems that the compiler has taken traditions about the large stones set up at Gilgal, the traditional entry point (Josh 4:20-24) and has associated them with Shechem, the site of the later covenant renewal ceremonies (Josh 8:30-35 and 24:1-28). Every covenant renewal ceremony is rooted in Israel's action on the first day of entry. Verses 4-7, as noted, locate the ceremony at Mt. Ebal near Shechem and describe an altar built according to the law in Exod 20:25, "And if you build me an altar of stone, you shall not build it of hewn stone." Sacrifice is to seal the covenant, both whole burnt offerings and communion sacrifices. In the latter sacrifice, part of the animal was consumed on the altar—transferred to the Lord's domain—and the rest was eaten by the worshipper. The Lord and his covenantal partners were united in a shared meal. Verse 8 resumes v. 3, making vv. 1-8 a unified section.

Verses 9-26 describe the rite to take place at the Shechem shrine with its inscribed stones and altar. Moses and the Levitical priests address the people in the spirit of 26:16-19. They have become the people of the Lord and therefore are to keep his commandments.

The ceremony in vv. 11-26 in which the people will be active respondents is not easy to imagine. Six tribes stand on each of the two mountains overlooking Shechem reciting the blessings and curses. They accept the consequences of their free response to the Lord who has invited them into union with him. There follow a series of twelve statements, each beginning with "cursed be the one who. . . ." The response of Israel to God was often summed up in ten or twelve member lists, of which the most famous was the Decalogue (lit. "list of ten"). Here it is twelve, dodecalogue, prefaced by a formulation of the great commandment. Why these particular laws were selected is not clear. Perhaps they are all actions done in secret and thus not likely to be punished by conventional means. At any rate six are duplicated also in the Covenant Code (Exod 20:22—23:33) and nine in the Holiness Code (Leviticus 17-26).

Strictly speaking, the statements are not curses, called down upon someone breaking the covenant, like the covenant curses of chap. 28. They are rather forbidden actions. The threat of divine punishment hangs over each. Nonetheless the chapter takes them as curses since according to v. 13, the six tribes use them to curse. The blessings spoken of in v. 12 are apparently the blessings that begin in chap. 28.

Chapter 27 displays Israel taking upon itself freely at the very moment of its arrival in the land the full consequences of its covenant with the Lord. Every generation is to stand before the Lord as at the first day and take upon itself the terrifying and ennobling consequences of being the Lord's people.

Section 5

BLESSINGS AND CURSES. END OF SECOND DISCOURSE.
28:1-68

> **28** "And if you obey the voice of the Lord your God, being careful to do all his commandments which I command you this day, the Lord your God will set you high above all the nations of the earth. ²And all these blessing shall come upon you and overtake you, if you obey the

voice of the Lord your God. ³Blessed shall you be in the city, and blessed shall you be in the field. ⁴Blessed shall be the fruit of your body, and the fruit of your ground, and the fruit of your beasts, the increase of your cattle, and the young of your flock. ⁵Blessed shall be your basket and your kneading-trough. ⁶Blessed shall you be when you come in, and blessed shall you be when you go out.

⁷"The Lord will cause your enemies who rise against you to be defeated before you; they shall come out against you one way, and flee before you seven ways. ¹³And the Lord will make you the head, and not the tail; and you shall tend upward only, and not downward; if you obey the commandments of the Lord your God, which I command you this day, being careful to do them, ¹⁴and if you do not turn aside from any of the words which I command you this day, to the right hand or to the left, to go after other gods to serve them.

¹⁵"But if you will not obey the voice of the Lord your God or be careful to do all his commandments and his statutes which I command you this day, then all these curses shall come upon you and overtake you. ¹⁶Cursed shall you be in the city, and cursed shall you be in the field. ¹⁷Cursed shall be your basket and your kneading-trough. ¹⁸Cursed shall be the fruit of your body, and the fruit of your ground, the increase of your cattle, and the young of your flock. ¹⁹Cursed shall you be when you come in, and cursed shall you be when you go out.

²⁰ "The Lord will send upon you curses, confusion, and frustration, in all that you undertake to do, until you are destroyed and perish quickly, on account of the evil of your doings, because you have forsaken me.

⁴⁵All these curses shall come upon you and pursue you and overtake you, till you are destroyed, because you did not obey the voice of the Lord your God, to keep his commandments and his statutes which he commanded you. ⁴⁶They shall be upon you as a sign and a wonder, and upon your descendants for ever.

⁴⁷"Because you did not serve the Lord your God with joyfulness and gladness of heart, by reason of the abundance of all things, ⁴⁸therefore you shall serve your enemies whom the Lord will send against you, in hunger and thirst, in nakedness, and in want of all things; and he will put a yoke of iron upon your neck, until he has destroyed you. ⁴⁹The Lord will bring a nation against you from afar, from the end of the earth, as swift as the eagle flies, a nation whose language you do not understand, ⁵⁰a nation of stern countenance, who shall not regard the person of the old or show favor to the young, ⁵¹and shall eat the offspring of your cattle and the fruit of your ground, until you are destroyed; who also shall not leave you grain, wine, or oil, the increase of your cattle or the young of your flock, until they have caused you to perish.

⁵⁸"If you are not careful to do all the words of this law which are written in this book, that you may fear this glorious and awful name, the Lord your God, ⁵⁹then the Lord will bring on you and your offspring extraordinary afflictions, afflictions severe and lasting, and sicknesses grievous and lasting.

Deuteronomy 4:44—28:68 forms a single speech of Moses modeled upon the covenant formulary. Behind chaps. 5-11 is the first element of that genre, the history of the lord's relationship to Israel with exhortation to fidelity; the stipulations are the second element (in chaps. 12-26). The blessings and curses, a third constant of the genre, are found in chap. 28 (after the anomalous chap. 27). As in many other ancient Near Eastern examples, the curses (vv. 15-68) far outnumber the blessings (vv. 1-14).

The modern reader may be puzzled by the cursed-filled conclusion to a speech which has up to this point focused on Israel's free response to a loving God. Curses as the finale in the covenant formulary are attested from the third millennium to the first. One always finds in the treaties, at a minimum, stipulations, god lists or invocations, and the curse formulae. The stipulations are imposed under oath and placed under the watchful eye of the gods. Violation of the oath will lead to the dire consequences described in the curses which the gods will oversee.

In the Israelite version of the curses in 28:15-68, the curses are portrayed both as natural forces turning against violators in vv. 15-19, 30-34, 38-46, and also as directly inflicted by the Lord in vv. 20-29, 36-37, 47-68. The texts are not mere legal documents; they reflect ceremonies. The parties stand before the gods and consciously take upon themselves the consequences of their acts. The gods will reward fidelity to the oaths sworn before them and will punish infidelity. The gods in the ancient Near East were often conceived as presenting themselves in natural phenomena, and as punishing by withholding the benefit of the natural good or by perverting it. Sometimes the god was not named. Often, however, the god inflicting the punishment was named. Deuteronomy 28 shows both modes of expression.

Both blessing and curse in the chapter are tied to the land. The land will or will not yield life to Israel according to their obedience. Yahweh will or will not afflict them with various forms of infertility or loss of land in military defeat on the same principle.

Is there any discernible outline to the vast chapter? Some scholars claim that the chapter is a patchwork of sections gradually added to reflect the actual conditions of exile. Though it is not a patchwork, it is possible that certain verses were added in the time of exile; the accurate detail served to remind Israel that their exile of 587-539 B.C. was the covenant curse taking effect. Verses 47-57 are no longer merely threats. They declare that the conditions are fulfilled which bring on the curses. "Because you did not serve the Lord your God with joyfulness and gladness of heart [i.e., freely and willingly] by reason of the abundance of all things. . . .therefore you shall serve your enemies whom the Lord will send against you. . . in want of all things." The verses may have been added during the second edition of the Deuteronomistic History at the time of the exile. (See "Introduction.") Even if additions have been made to this chapter, an outline is clearly visible. We follow the analysis of Dennis McCarthy, which indicates careful structuring between conditions ("A" in the outline) and results ("B" in the outline):

I. Blessings: 1-14
    A. Conditions governing blessings, 1-2
    B. Results: the blessings, 3-13a
        1. Impersonal formulations, 3-6
        2. Personal: Yahweh acts, 7-13a
    A^1. Condition repeated, 13b-14
II. Curses: 15-68
    A. Conditions governing curses, 15
    B. Results: the curses, 16-44
        1. Impersonal formulations, 16-19
        2. Personal: Yahweh acts, 20-29
            a. Development of topic sentence in 29 by a different agent, 30-34
        2^1. Personal: Yahweh acts, 35-37
            a^1. Development of topic sentence in 37 by a different agent, 38-44
    A^1. Condition becomes fact: conclusion, 45-46
    A^2. Condition becomes fact: introduction, 47
    B^1. Results: punishment, 48-57
        1. Personal: Yahweh acts, 48a-49a
            a. Development: enemy and his acts, 49b-57
    A^3. Condition governing punishment, 58
    B^2. Results: Personal acts of Yahweh, 59-68

We comment now on some of the details. The blessings (vv. 1-14) as well as the curses revolve about the land, the land as fertile, as protected from enemies, as a place where Israel's special choice by the Lord will be seen by the nations. The last point, Israel's priority among the nations, is emphasized three times, vv. 1, 9-10, 12b-13. Israel as Yahweh's special possession (32:8) will be "high (*'elyôn*) above all the nations of the earth" (v. 1) just as Yahweh is high (*'elyôn*) above all the heavenly powers. The people however must remain holy, i.e. close to Yahweh, to share in his preeminence. Blessings in the city and the field, the fruit of your body and of the ground will overtake Israel, bent on doing good (v. 2 and, conversely, vv. 15 and 45). In vv. 3-6 the blessings are presented in opposites: city-field, basket-kneading trough, coming in-going out. The literary device is known as merism (from Greek *meros*, "part"), in which aspects are mentioned to express totality. Verse 4 which associates human offspring, animal offspring and the produce of the soil—the word "fruit" being used for all three—reminds us that the Israelites did not objectify nature but saw continuity in life. Yahweh's blessing enhanced all life in the world.

In the second group of blessings (vv. 7-14), Yahweh acts directly upon the people. The repetition of the blessings in vv. 7-14—of v. 1 in vv. 9-10, 13-14, and of v. 4 in v. 11—illustrates the redundancy of religious oratory. Verses 12b-13a depict Israel as raised above the nations because of the rich blessings of fertility and protection against enemies. Israel will rise to the top of the nations (cf., 15:6). Verses 13-14 remind the hearers that Moses communicates the authentic commands of Yahweh to the exclusion of other gods.

What was said of the blessings applies in large measure to the curses in vv. 15-68. The curses even more than the blessings display the conventions of the curses in ancient treaties. Even the order of certain curses is conventional. For example v. 35, the plague of boils, has nothing to do with its immediate context of vv. 30-34 and 36 but does have a relation to vv. 27-29. It seems that the traditional order overrode immediate context. Some of the blessings of vv. 1-14 are explicitly reversed: vv. 15-19 reverse vv. 2-6; vv. 23-24 reverse v. 12; v. 25 reverses v.7; vv. 25, 37, 46 reverse vv. 1, 9-10, 13-14; vv. 43-44 reverse vv. 12b-13a; v. 45 reverses v. 2. The parallels are not mathematically precise. In general the curses cut Israel off from the life that is in the land, either by afflicting them with sickness or by leaving them defenseless before their enemies. Especially the matched sections of vv. 30-34 and vv. 38-44 show Israel looking on powerlessly while its links to the land are broken. Verse 46 marks the end of a stage in the curses, with v. 45 deliberately pointing the attentive reader back to v. 1.

In v. 47 the speech moves from threat to actuality. The horror is now being experienced, "because you did not serve the Lord your God. . . therefore you shall serve your enemies. . . " As noted, these last curses probably reflect the bitter realities of the Babylonian exile, even though the language is found in treaties of every age. In vv. 47-57 Yahweh uses as instrument of punishment a strong and vicious nation which will unleash upon Israel the horrors of war including the horrors of an extended siege in vv. 52-57. In the biblical view every nation has a "god" which it serves. Israel served Pharaoh in Egypt before it served Yahweh in Canaan. Now the people will fall back into serving another suzerain, the nation which Yahweh will send against them (vv. 47-51).

Verses 58-68 further elaborate the curses. Verse 58 refers to "the book," as does v. 61, showing that this speech of Moses was read by an Israel of a later age. The old sacred promise to the patriarchs of a multitude of progeny in Gen 15:5 is turned into a curse in vv. 62-63. The old action of exodus-conquest is now reversed into plagues against Israel rather than against Egypt (vv. 60-61) and a scattering among the nations rather than a gathering into the one land (v. 64). The psychological pains will be great (vv. 67-68). The people end up as slaves in Egypt in v. 68, the ultimate reversal of Yahweh's great work of rescue unto freedom.

The seriousness of the bond between Yahweh and Israel could not be more graphically portrayed. The intensity of life with the Lord, the horror of life away from the Lord—both find memorable expression in this powerful final speech.

THE THIRD SPEECH.
29:1—32:52

"These are the words" introduces the third of the four major segments of the book. The other introductions are 1:1, 4:44 and 33:1. Not all segments of this section were originally together; their unity is redactional. Chapters 29-30 now form a single speech of Moses, making use of elements originally at home in the covenant formulary. Chapter 31 is a composite, containing duplicate accounts of the installation of Joshua and duplicate introductions to the Song of Moses. Chapter 32 is the Song of Moses, a venerable poem that has been incorporated into this section. The redactor however has seen unity underlying the diversity. The installation of Joshua as Moses' successor and the provision for the preservation and reading of the law both belong to an account of the covenant. In addition, the vocabulary and structure of the Song of Moses has profoundly influenced the preceding chapters. The redactor, probably the second editor of the Deuteronomistic History, alerts the reader to the coherence of these chapters and to their relation to the rest of the book by the title, "These are the words."

Section 1.
Assurance to Israel: The Covenant
Still Offers Life
29:1—30:20

²And Moses summoned all Israel and said to them: "You have seen all that the Lord did before your eyes in the land of Egypt, to Pharaoh and to all his servants and to all his land, ³the great trials which your eyes saw, the signs, and those great wonders; ⁴but to this day the Lord has not given you a mind to understand, or eyes to see, or ears to hear. ⁵I have led you forty years in the wilderness; your clothes have not worn out upon you, and your sandals have not worn off your feet; ⁶you have not eaten bread, and you have not drunk wine or strong drink; that you may know that I am the Lord your God. ⁷And when you came to this place, Sihon the king of Heshbon and Og the king of Bashan came out against us to battle, but we defeated them; ⁸we took their land, and gave it for an inheritance to the Reubenites, the Gadites, and the half-tribe of the Manassites. ⁹Therefore be careful to do the words of this covenant, that you may prosper in all that you do.

²⁴yea, all the nations would say, 'Why has the Lord done thus to this land? What means the heat of this great anger?'' ²⁵Then men would say, 'It is because they forsook the covenant of the Lord, the God of their fathers, which he made with them when he brought them out of the land of Egypt, ²⁶and went and served other gods and worshiped them, gods whom they had not known and whom he had not allotted to them; ²⁷therefore the anger of the Lord was kindled against this land, bringing upon it all the curses written in this book; ²⁸and the Lord uprooted them from their land in anger and fury and great wrath, and cast them into another land, as at this day.'

30 "And when all these things come upon you, the blessing and the curse, which I have set before you, and you call them to mind among all the nations where the Lord your God has driven you, ²and return to the Lord your God, you and your children, and obey his voice in all that I command you this day, with all your heart and with all your soul; ³then the Lord your God will restore your fortunes, and have compassion upon you, and he will gather you again from all the peoples where the Lord your God has scattered you.

¹⁵"See, I have set before you this day life and good, death and evil. ¹⁶If you obey the commandments of the Lord your God which I command you this day, by loving the Lord your God, by walking in his ways, and by keeping his commandments and his statutes and his ordinances, then you shall live and multiply, and the Lord your God will bless you in the land which you are entering to take possession of it. ¹⁷But if your heart turns away, and you will not hear, but are drawn away to worship other gods and serve them, ¹⁸I declare to you this day, that you shall perish; you shall not live long in the land which you are going over the Jordan to enter and possess. ¹⁹I call heaven and earth to witness against you this day, that I have set before you life and death, blessing and curse; therefore choose life, that you and your descendants may live, ²⁰loving the Lord your God, obeying his voice, and cleaving to him; for that means life to you and length of days, that you may dwell in the land which the Lord swore to your fathers, to Abraham, to Isaac, and to Jacob, to give them."

Within chaps. 29-32, the third section of Deuteronomy, chaps. 29-30 are a single sermon of Moses. It is possible that elements of it once existed independently of the present speech. Chapters 29:21-28, for example, speak of the curses that have come over the whole land, whereas the preceding vv. 16-20 have spoken of the Lord's punishing a single unfaithful person or tribe. Verse 29 is a gloss, inspired perhaps by the Song of Moses (32:34-35). Most scholars see these chapters as independent sections loosely related to one another.

Diverse as the components may be in their origin, a single scheme is discernible. Each one of the elements is found in the covenant formularies of the time, though not necessarily in the order in which they appear in this speech. The historical prologue is found in 29:2-9, the list of parties in 29:10-15, stipulations in 29:16-21, curses in 29:22-28, blessings in 30:1-10, curses and blessings mixed in 30:15-18, and invocation of witnesses in v. 19. Exhortations such as 30:11-14 and 19b-20 occur in some formularies. The chapter is not itself a covenant formulary, but a speech that draws upon the formulary tradition to persuade hearers to be loyal to the Lord.

The introduction in 29:1 declares the whole section—the speech of Moses, the installation of Joshua and the Song—to be "the words of the covenant." Further, this covenant is said to be distinct from that covenant made at Horeb (Sinai) in that it restates the original ceremony and experience.

The first section of the speech, vv. 2-9, recites the history of the Lord's benefits, the exodus-conquest. Verses 2-3 speak of the freedom from slavery won by the plagues and the victory at the sea, "the great trials which your eyes saw, the signs, and those great wonders." The divine guidance through the wilderness to the land is emphasized by miraculous details. Clothing and sandals did not wear out. Israel did not have ordinary food and drink but manna, quail, and water from the rock so they would acknowledge it was the Lord who nourished Israel in the wilderness. Verse 7 describes the conquest. As in chaps. 2-3, the Transjordanian area is seen as the first stage in the conquest. The defeat of Kings Sihon and Og and the distribution of their land to the two and a half tribes presages the full scale conquest under Joshua. The sermon is thus prefaced by the story of what the Lord has done for his people and how he has come to be their suzerain. The exodus-conquest is the essence of that story. For Israel to recite the story is to confess that its whole existence is owed to the Lord. The historical recital begins with a sober warning that the people have not to this day understood the full import of Yahweh's acts for them, and ends with an exhortation to observe the covenant (v. 9).

In the next section, the parties to the covenant are identified. In Joshua 24, a text similar to this one, the order is reversed. There the parties are mentioned in the very first verse, *before* the historical recital. Here the parties are addressed in the second person (as opposed to the third person in Joshua 24) after hearing of Yahweh's deeds for them in vv. 2-9, a touch adding urgency to this speech. Moses' concern for future generations in v. 14 is a constant theme of the entire section.

Verses 16-21 adapt the covenant tradition of curses to make clear that divine punishment will fall upon those who worship the gods of the foreign lands. Even a single individual could bring about the downfall of the whole people by his or her sin. Joshua 7 describes how the sin of an individual, Achan, brought punishment upon all. Here each Israelite is warned that even secretly-held allegiances to idols would make that person a root bearing bitter fruit for the nation. The curses written in the book—the existence of the book of the covenant is presupposed—would settle upon the guilty party.

Though the guilty individual, family, or tribe would be set apart for punishment, the whole land nonetheless will feel the brunt of the curses. As in Joshua 7, Achan may be singled out by lot for punishment, but all the people suffer. Similar curses are expressed in 1 Kgs 9:8-9 where also in a covenant context foreigners answer the question, "Why has the Lord done thus to this land and this house?" "Because they forsook the Lord their God who brought their fathers out of the land of Egypt, and laid hold on other gods, and worshiped them and served them; therefore the Lord has brought all this evil upon them." The scene with its question and answer dramatizing the real possibility of destruction is also found in Assyrian texts referring to treaties. In this chapter of Deuteronomy later generations of Israelites as well as foreigners upon seeing the devastated land ask the question in v. 22, "Why has the Lord done this?" They answer that it is not fate or the military superiority of the nations but the Lord's wrath, i.e. his turning away from Israel because of covenant breach. The Lord is not a neutral force but a personal being, capable of rising to heights of wrath (3 times repeated) when his offer of love is spurned by his people's turn to other gods. Yahweh's rival gods, mentioned in vv. 17, 18, and 26, are termed in v. 26, "gods whom they had not known and whom he had not allotted to them." "Known" in the first part of the phrase means "confessed." The people have never recognized and confessed the presence and power of these gods in the events by which they became the Lord's people, as they have of the Lord, as in v. 6, "that you may know that I am the Lord your God." The second part of the phrase, "(the gods) whom he had not allotted to them" refers to the primordial act by which the Most High allotted to each of the sons of God (in the Israelite conception, pale reflections of the gods of polytheism) a particular nation or people, but keeping Israel for himself (32:8-9). Rejection of the Most High with his gift of land can only lead to the loss of that land (v. 28).

Verse 29, which teaches that secret or non-public things belong to the Lord, is a gloss. It likewise may reflect the Song, 32:34-35, that vengeance upon the enemies is stored up with the Lord. In the Song the promise of vengeance comes after the unleashing of the curses in 32:21-25. The gloss assures Israel that while vengeance upon their enemies is not their responsibility, it *is* their responsibility to heed the warnings just heard and to repent. The human act of repentance and not the divine act of vengeance is the appropriate action for them and their children.

Next, 30:1-10 draws on the blessing vocabulary of the treaty formularies to show that if Israel repents the Lord will bring them home, and with inner renewal, a "circumcised heart," that will assure obedience and prosperity. It is assumed that the curses of 29:20-28 have taken effect:

Israel has sinned and consequently has been driven from the land. But even in exile Israel can remember the possibilities still inherent in the covenant and return to the Lord. The Hebrew word for "return" or "repentance," *shûb,* is important in prophetic preaching especially in the Exile and thereafter in Jewish tradition. In response to the Israelites' repentance, Yahweh will "repent," or restore *(shûb)* the fortunes of Israel (30:3). Restoring the fortunes of an exiled Israel means bringing them back from captivity, from the uttermost parts of the world (vv. 4-5).

But will it not be inevitable that even a restored Israel will once again get caught in the sequence of sin and punishment? To break the chain of inevitability Israel will be transformed by circumcision of the heart. The phrase, used before in 10:16, probably means to strip from the heart, the seat of intelligence, the overlay of flesh that makes it dull and irresponsive. Israel can begin a new life in the land with a better possibility of obedience than in the past. (See also Jer 31:31-34.) The Lord will make the land fertile and so prosper the people (v. 9, and 28:4, 11), a Deuteronomic touch. The section ends with an exhortation, a common device to end units in Deuteronomic speeches (cf., 29:9).

Verses 11-14 is an exhortation designed to assure the Israelite, awed perhaps by the enormous consequences of his or her response to the words of the covenant, that the commandment is within reach. The rhetorical development is effective. The word is neither in heaven nor beyond the sea; it is received from Moses' mouth into the hearer's heart where it can be a principle of prospering activity.

The last section combines covenantal blessings and curses with invocation of witnesses to form one of the most compelling addresses in the entire Bible. Twice Moses says that he sets before his hearers, the whole people from elder to infant, freeman to slave, the present generation and the future (29:10-15) their awesome choice—life or death. Because the speech is liturgical, i.e. done "before Yahweh," life and death has a specific meaning. Life in the liturgical context is proximity to the Lord, "to dwell in the house of the Lord [or in his land] all the days of my life" (Ps 27:4). Death means to be absent from the Lord, and from the land where he dwells. Blessings and curses mean essentially the same as life and death—to dwell with the Lord and enjoy him through his land, or to be cast out of his land to live in the lands of strange gods. The act of fidelity or infidelity to the Lord in vv. 15-18 is the determinant of blessings or curses. All important moral decisions are reduceable to either of the two choices.

In v. 19, Moses calls upon heaven and earth to witness the people's choice. In the covenant formularies of polytheistic cultures, the gods were called upon to observe the oaths so as to reward and avenge accordingly. Sometimes the list of deities believed active in a region included pairs of cosmic elements, mountains and hills, springs and wells, sun and moon, heaven and earth. Israel of course could invoke no god but Yahweh but did sometimes retain a pair like heaven and earth which they must have interpreted in an impersonal sense (Isa 1:2; Mic 6:1-2; Jer 2:12; Ps 50:4; Deut 4:26, 31:28). The cosmic pair heightened the significance of the action. In a memorable phrase Israel is urged to choose life, to choose deliberately to enter the sphere where blessings will be given. It is a rejection of death and an end to the absence of the Lord. It can be paraphrased as obeying the voice of the Lord in the voice of Moses in the liturgical ceremony, as cleaving to the Lord, as bringing enhancement to daily life, and safe dwelling in the land where ones' ancestors have lived (vv. 19-20).

Moses has emphasized in his speech that his words are addressed not only to the generation of Moab but especially to later Israelites. Note that only in liturgical celebration "today" do the people realize fully the meaning of past saving acts (29:4 and 6b). The emphasis is on the sons and daughters of the present generation in 29:14-15; 30:2, 6, 19. Israel is always to see itself at the threshold of the promised land hearing the words of the covenant that brings life. It has only two choices.

Section 2.
Provisions for the Law
after Moses' Death
31:1-29

²And he said to them, "I am a hundred and twenty
years old this day; I am no longer able to go out and
come in. The Lord has said to me,'You shall not go over
this Jordan.' ³The Lord your God himself will go over
before you; he will destroy these nations before you, so
that you shall dispossess them; and Joshua will go over
at your head, as the Lord has spoken.

⁷Then Moses summoned Joshua, and said to him in
the sight of all Israel, "Be strong and of good courage;
for you shall go with this people into the land which the
Lord has sworn to their fathers to give them; and you
shall put them in possession of it. ⁸It is the Lord who
goes before you; he will be with you, he will not fail you
or forsake you; do not fear or be dismayed."

⁹And Moses wrote this law, and gave it to the priests
the sons of Levi, who carried the ark of the covenant of
the Lord, and to all the elders of Israel. ¹⁰And Moses
commanded them, "At the end of every seven years, at
the set time of the year of release, at the feast of booths,
¹¹when all Israel comes to appear before the Lord your
God at the place which he will choose, you shall read
this law before all Israel in their hearing.

²⁴When Moses had finished writing the words of this
law in a book, to the very end, ²⁵Moses commanded the
Levites who carried the ark of the covenant of the Lord,
²⁶"Take this book of the law, and put it by the side of
the ark of the covenant of the Lord your God, that it
may be there for a witness against you. ²⁷For I know
how rebellious and stubborn you are; behold, while I
am yet alive with you, today you have been rebellious
against the Lord; how much more after my death!
²⁸Assemble to me all the elders of your tribes, and your

officers, that I may speak these words in their ears and call heaven and earth to witness against them. ²⁹For I know that after my death you will surely act corruptly, and turn aside from the way which I have commanded you; and in the days to come evil will befall you, because you will do what is evil in the sight of the Lord, provoking him to anger through the work of your hands."

The final redactor has included this chapter in the third section of Deuteronomy (29:1—32:52) which is introduced by the title, "These are the words" in 29:1. The redactor has seen in this originally disparate section a unity arising from the covenant formulary which he is using as a model: historical review, blessings and curses, exhortations. Other elements from the covenant tradition appear also in chap. 31, provision for succession of the leader and the storage and public reading of the text, which unify this chapter as well.

The redactor has arranged the diverse material with great skill to make his point: the work of Moses will be continued in two ways—in the person of Joshua and by the written law (summarized in the Song of Moses, chap. 32).

The modern reader is likely to be confused by the diversity; hence the structure of the chapter must be discussed in detail. The first section in the chapter is vv. 1-8. It has already been suggested in the commentary on 3:18-28 that 31:1-8 continues directly chap. 3 to form the introduction to the first edition of the Deuteronomistic History and was itself further continued in Joshua 1. In 3:18-28, Moses commands the two and a half tribes who had already been allotted their land in Transjordan to go over with their brethren to fight with them for the land that yet remains (3:18-20). Moses then makes a last great plea to God to be allowed to go over with the people but is rebuffed and told that Joshua will lead in his place (3:23-28). This last scene is private. Its public counterpart is in the ceremony of commission in chap. 31. "So Moses went to speak these words

to all Israel," is the most likely translation of 31:1, though
the Greek version and a Qumran scroll read, "And Moses
finished speaking."

In vv. 1-8 Moses publicly confirms what he had privately
experienced: Joshua will lead the people, i.e., lead in holy
war and in apportionment of the land (v. 7b). Moses
begins by reminding the people of his old age and consequent incapacity to continue his work. "Go out" and
"come in" in v. 2 is a merism, the mention of the two ends
of the spectrum for the whole. Verse 3 reminds us that the
real leader is Yahweh. Joshua is simply a delegate to lead in
holy war across the Jordan as Moses did in Transjordan
(vv. 4-5). In holy war it is crucial to believe that Yahweh
with his heavenly army goes against the enemy. One must
go out with a reckless courage based on the belief that the
reliable Lord advances with one (v. 6).

Verses 7-8 is the commission of Joshua, expressed
through a series of imperatives commanding typical conduct, like the imperatives in the commission of the judges
and officers in 16:18—17:7.

The next section is more complicated. Scholars rightly
have seen that vv. 9-13 about Moses' writing down the law
with a view to its later preaching is directly continued by
vv. 24-29, the actual reading of it to the "elders of your
tribes, and your officers," representatives of the people.
Once again, imperative verbs show the institution of a
custom. This latter section, like vv. 9-13 which it continues, is generally considered Deuteronomistic, probably
from the author who produced 4:1-40. Scholars generally
recognize a second account of the installation of Joshua in
vv. 14-15 + 23 and attribute it to J-E, the old epic source.
This second account of the installation continues the old
epic tradition that placed Moses and his servant Joshua in
time of crisis at the Tent of Meeting to meet Yahweh in the
pillar of cloud (cf. Exod 33:7-11). In the crisis of transfer-
ring the power of leadership, Yahweh speaks authoritative-
ly from the pillar of cloud to appoint Joshua.

The third section in vv. 14-22, from a source different

from the preceding two, introduces the Song of chap. 32 as a "witness" (vv. 19, 21) against the people. The Song will show that the many evils and troubles that come upon Israel are the result of their sin. It serves as an introduction to the Song itself.

Out of this diversity the redactor (who was as aware as we are of the diversity) wove a coherent picture. The first section (vv. 1-8) makes public the private revelation to Moses that he is about to be replaced by Joshua. The Lord will still go ahead of Israel across the Jordan but with Joshua as his delegate. Joshua's attitude of confidence in the divine leadership is paradigmatic for all Israel. His leadership is not so much military skill as it is faith in the Lord who goes on before Israel as a warrior (vv. 6-8).

For Moses to install a successor to himself in the task of leading the people to take possession of the land is only one provision for Israel's welfare. The other provision is the law (vv. 9-13). It must be written down and read periodically so that Israel of every generation might learn to do it. It was not unusual to find in an ancient Near Eastern treaty a clause providing for its regular reading. A copy of the law is to be stored with the ark upon which Yahweh was believed to dwell. Every seventh year, "you shall read this law before all Israel" (v. 11).

Verses 14-15, which describe the appointment of Joshua at the Tent of Meeting, authenticates Joshua as law speaker, just as vv. 1-8 authenticated Joshua as conqueror and distributor of the land.

Verse 16, "Behold you are about to sleep with your fathers," resumes v. 14, "behold the days approach when you must die." Resumption is a frequent device of biblical narrative to get back to the main point after a digression. The death of Moses on the eve of entry to life in the new land poses an acute problem. How will Israel encounter the covenantal blessings and curses without the presence of Moses? In vv. 16-22 the answer is that Moses leaves behind a witness, the Song of chap. 32, that contains the whole covenant pattern: Yahweh's gracious deed and Israel's rebellion (32:1-18), the unleashing of curses (32:19-25), the ultimate rescue of Israel and the punishment of their enemies (vv. 26-43). Chapter 31:16-22 (also vv. 26-29) focuses only on the middle part of the Song, the rebellion of Israel and their punishment (32:7-25). Moses wants to leave a simple but memorable witness to his people of the consequences of their infidelity in the land. He leaves them his Song.

Yahweh tells Moses that the people will be un-faithful—violating the great commandment by worshiping other deities. The language of whoring in v. 16 implies both the fidelity to its Lord that should characterize Israel's affections, and the sexual nature of the rites of worship of other gods. The covenant curses—described in chap. 28—come upon them through the Lord's anger, ex-plained as the withdrawal of his *panim,* his "face" or presence (v. 17). At the crucial moment of punishment, the Song is to become a witness to them that what has befallen them is truly from the curses of the covenant. Witnesses were often invoked in ancient treaties, customarily the gods or natural phenomena enshrining divine power, to witness the original transaction and to punish or reward according to its observance. In an Israelite shift, the Song itself has been made into the witness, allowing the people to encounter their punishing Lord in their infidelity.

The Song has powerfully shaped vv. 16-22. To mention only a few instances: "evils" of 32:23 occurs in vv. 17 (2x), 21; "to hide the face from them" in 32:20 occurs in vv. 17-18; the description of the holy land as filled with rich food in 32:13-14 occurs in v. 20. Moses writes the Song on the same day as he writes the law (v. 22, cf. vv. 9 and 24). The Song thus serves as a kind of miniaturized law, a readily available instrument of confrontation. The next verse, v. 23, extends the use of the Song to Joshua, Moses' successor.

The last section of the chapter, vv. 24-29, is also con-cerned in its own way with the problem raised for Israel's covenant fidelity by Moses' departure. The law, chaps.

5-28, is deposited by the Ark of the Covenant. The Decalogue is contained inside (10:2, 5). The thought is somber. The rebellion of the people is so ingrained and so dangerous in its consequences that Moses even in his last hours must issue a warning to the people through their representatives, the tribal elders and their officers. He calls upon the ancient treaty pairs, heaven and earth, to witness Israel's every act. Even the Israelite's most secret acts of worship to other gods will be visible to the all-encompassing heaven and earth.

These verses, like vv. 16-22, also introduce the Song as a witness. They do so not only by their position immediately before chap. 32. Their invocation of heaven and earth as witnesses in v. 28 is repeated in 32:1, "Give ear, O heavens, and I will speak; and let the earth hear the words of my mouth." The Song functions to let generations subsequent to Moses know that evils come upon them from their offended covenant Lord.

Section 3.
The Song of Moses
31:30—32:52

32 "Give ear, O heavens, and I will
    speak;
and let the earth hear the words of
    my mouth.
²May my teaching drop as the rain,
    my speech distil as the dew,
as the gentle rain upon the tender
    grass,
    and as the showers upon the herb.
³For I will proclaim the name of the
    LORD.
    Ascribe greatness to our God!

⁷Remember the days of old,
    consider the years of many genera-
    tions;

ask your father, and he will show you;
   your elders, and they will tell you.
⁸When the Most High gave to the na-
      tions their inheritance,
   when he separated the sons of men,
he fixed the bounds of the peoples
   according to the number of the sons
      of God.
⁹For the LORD'S portion is his people,
   Jacob his allotted heritage.

¹⁰"He found him in a desert land,
   and in the howling waste of the wil-
      derness;
   he encircled him, he cared for him,
      he kept him as the apple of his eye.
¹¹Like an eagle that stirs up its nest,
      that flutters over its young,
   spreading out its wings, catching them,
      bearing them on its pinions,
¹²the LORD alone did lead him,
   and there was no foreign god with
      him.
¹³He made him ride on the high places
      of the earth,
   and he ate the produce of the field;
and he made him suck honey out of
      the rock,
   and oil out of the flinty rock.
¹⁴Curds from the herd, and milk from
      the flock,
   with fat of lambs and rams,
   herds of Bashan and goats,
with the finest of the wheat—
   and of the blood of the grape you
      drank wine.

¹⁷They sacrificed to demons which were
      no gods,
   to gods they had never known,
to new gods that had come in of late,
   whom your fathers had never
      dreaded.

[19]"The LORD saw it, and spurned them,
because of the provocation of his
sons and his daughters.
[20]And he said, 'I will hide my face from
them,
I will see what their end will be,
for they are a perverse generation,
children in whom is no faithfulness.
[21]They have stirred me to jealousy with
what is no god;
they have provoked me with their
idols.
So I will stir them to jealousy with
those who are no people;
I will provoke them with a foolish
nation.

[26]I would have said, "I will scatter them
afar,
I will make the remembrance of
them cease from among men,"
[27]had I not feared provocation by the
enemy,
lest their adversaries should judge
amiss,
lest they should say, "Our hand is triumphant,
the LORD has not wrought all this." '

[36]For the LORD will vindicate his people
and have compassion on his servants,
when he sees that their power is gone,
and there is none remaining, bond or
free.
[37]Then he will say, 'Where are their gods,
the rock in which they took refuge,
[38]who ate the fat of their sacrifices,
and drank the wine of their drink
offering?
Let them rise up and help you,
let them be your protection!

³⁹" 'See now that I, even I, am he,
　　and there is no god beside me;
　I kill and I make alive;
　　I wound and I heal;
　　and there is none that can deliver out
　　　of my hand.
⁴⁰For I lift up my hand to heaven,
　　and swear, As I live for ever,
⁴¹if I whet my glittering sword,
　　and my hand takes hold on judg-
　　　ment,
　I will take vengeance on my adver-
　　　saries,
　　and will requite those who hate me.
⁴²I will make my arrows drunk with
　　　blood,
　　and my sword shall devour flesh—
　with the blood of the slain and the
　　　captives,
　　from the long-haired heads of the
　　　enemy.'

⁴³"Praise his people, O you nations;
　　for he avenges the blood of his serv-
　　　ants,
　and takes vengeance on his adversaries,
　　and makes expiation for the land of
　　　his people."

The Song of Moses, one of the most powerful poems in the Bible on the Lord's choice of his people, is the climax of the third speech in Deuteronomy, chaps. 29-32. The sermon of chaps. 29-30 and the installation ceremonies of chap. 31 have prepared the reader for the Song. The drama expressed in the sermon is the same as that of the Song: in the face of the gracious deeds that brought Israel into existence (29:2-9 // 32:7-14), Israel rebels (29:16-28 // 32:15-25), but the Lord stands ready to rescue his devastated people (30:1-20 // 32:36-43). It is quite possible that the structure of the venerable Song has shaped the

structure of the sermon. The drama of both Song and sermon at any rate moves along similar lines: gracious deed,
rebellion and punishment, new offer of life in the covenant. Both make a powerful appeal to a community con-
scious of having been cursed through its disobedience.

Chapter 31 also leads to the Song. Some Song
vocabulary appears in 31:16-22 (see the commentary).
More importantly, 31:16-22 and 24-29 describe the Song as
summarizing the law so as to confront Israel both with its
curses and blessings.

The Song itself follows a pattern discernible in another
long poem, Psalm 78, with which it can be usefully compared. Psalm 78 has two recitals of sacred history.

	Psalm 78		Deuteronomy 32
Introduction	1-11		1- 6
	First Recital	Second Recital	
Gracious Act	12-16	42-55	7-14
Rebellion	17-20	56-58	15-18
Divine Anger & Punishment	21-32	59-64	19-25
Day of Judgment & New Beginning	(33-41)	65-72	26-43

The above analysis suggests that the purpose of the poem is
to convince Israel that the punishment it has undergone for
its infidelity is not the end of the covenant. The offer of
life still holds.

To leave the aim so abstractly stated would be to miss
the rich development of ideas. To the rhetoric of the poem
we now turn. Verses 1-6 is the introduction, in three sections of 6 lines each (vv. 1-2, 3-4, 5-6). The speaker calls
upon heaven and earth to hear or witness his words.
Heaven and earth are invoked here, as they were in 30:19
and 31:28, to witness the original covenant; hence to watch
over its observance. Let the whole world hear the legal
statement of Moses regarding the covenant relationship of
Israel and Yahweh its Lord! Verses 3-4 are more specific

than appears at first reading. The speaker asks the congregation to give to Yahweh the recognition and honor he deserves. "His work' and"his ways" of v. 4 refer to the activity and acomplishments of the Lord in the world which prove his divinity amid the competing claims of other deities. Among the gods of the polytheistic culture, Yahweh alone can be counted on ("faithfulness" in v. 4b); he is not capricious and acts according to his justice. In the ancient world, the people of a god reflected on earth, "among the nations," the god's rank and standing in the heavenly world. Verses 5-6 declare that Israel fails to recognize their God; that is the meaning of "folly" here and in the other uses of the word in vv. 15 ("scoffed" in *RSV*), 21, 28-29. Not recognizing that Yahweh is their father (the epithet means creator here) they are not his children and thus cannot reflect adequately his priority in the heavenly world.

Verses 7-14 illustrate how the Lord is Israel's creator and hence has a claim upon their allegiance. "Remember the days of old" in v. 7 does not mean simply to recall a forgotten fact but to recite publicly the classic saving story, presumably in the liturgical assembly. In Ps 77, a lament over a national distress seriously threatening the existence of the nation, the assembly "remembers," "recites," and "sings," (the *RSV* of Ps 77:11-12 does not adequately translate the verbs) the ancient founding deed that made Israel a people. That deed is described in Ps 77:13-20: Yahweh's manifestation in the heavens (v. 13) and on earth (v. 14) of his power by leading Jacob and Joseph through the waters by the hands of Moses and Aaron (vv. 15-20). Ps 74:12-17 is similar. So also in the Song of Moses: In time of crisis Israel realizes itself by telling its story.

The story in the Song, though conforming to the traditional pattern of divine rescue and procession to the land, has its own unique coloring. It begins not on earth but in heaven, in the assembly of the gods where every important issue of world order was decided. The agenda for the meeting is the assignment of nations to the protection and patronage of the "sons of God." In the polytheistic context they are the group of deities sired by the senior god and his consort. Here they are simply heavenly figures subordinate to the Most High. Israel in the early period kept to the conventional ways of speaking about God. Each of the deities, called in other texts "the seventy sons of El," is assigned a nation, but the Most High (an appellation for Yahweh in contrast to the subordinate heavenly figures) reserves Israel for himself.

The manner in which Yahweh the Most High actually chooses Israel as his own "portion" on earth, in history, is detailed in vv. 10-14. Yahweh says that no other god assisted; he alone created them. The implications of this will be drawn out later. Verse 13 speaks of the arrival at the Lord's holy mountain. It can be paraphrased, "He brought him up to the top of the mountain," i.e. the land of Canaan itself, or perhaps the Lord's mountain shrine in the midst of the land. Israel is led into the paradisiacal peace of their God's mountain shrine. Isa 11:6-9 speaks of "my holy mountain" where tamed nature serves humankind, in a new Eden. Other references to the fertile center include Pss 46, 48, 76 and Ezek 40-48. The fertility of the mountain in vv. 13-14 is the opposite of the murderous infertility of the desert in v. 10.

The above poem is but another version of the redemption of Israel from Egypt and the conquest of the land. It is also a version of the creation of Israel. A creation narrative (better: account of cosmogony) in the ancient Near East differed in at least three respects from modern conceptions of creation: (1) the emergent was a structured human society rather than an unpeopled universe; (2) interest was often centered on only one aspect of the world, e.g. how kingship arose or marriage or the alphabet, rather than on the whole universe; (3) the creation process is conflictual involving personal wills rather than evolutionary and impersonal. Whether one calls the little account of vv. 8-14 redemption or creation, the important point is that it shows how Israel owes its total existence as a protected and prosperous people to the Lord alone.

Israel's response to grace is rebellion, vv. 15-18. Its abundant food only makes it grossly insensitive to the Lord who created it. It turns instead to worship the gods of the land who had no share in its origin.

The Lord did not create his people with the dispassionateness of the Aristotelian prime mover. He had passionately entered into covenant; hence their rebellion leaves him furious (vv. 19-25). "I will hide my face," i.e. withdraw my presence, he declares. Then with a typical Eastern feel for the appropriate punishment afflicts Israel with a "no people" as they afflicted him with a "no god." The "no people" is unidentifiable. A number of the curses in chap. 28 are carried out by an enemy army (Deut 28:49-57) and they are so here. The enemy king as the executor of the Lord's wrath against his own people is common in the Old Testament, e.g. the Asssyrian king in Isa 10:5-19 + 14:24-27 and the enemy from the north in Jer 1:13-14; 4:5-31; 5:15-17; 6:1-5, etc. Typically the enemy king is unaware that his defeat of Israel is due to Yahweh's will and credits himself with the victory. The Assyrian king says, "By the strength of my hand I have done it . . . I have removed the boundaries of the peoples. . . .My hand has found like a nest the wealth of the peoples. . . ." (Isa 10:13-14). Yahweh fears such a prideful boast of the enemy in 32:27, "Our hand is triumphant, Yahweh has not wrought all this."

The wrath of God is portrayed in conventional terms in vv. 22-25 (cf., Ps 78:21, 31, 59-64). Though the chief instrument of punishment is an enemy army, the destruction can be portrayed as famine, blasting heat, and poisonous animals like the original state of chaos before Israel existed (v. 10).

But Israel remains, by divine decree, Yahweh's own, designed to display his glory. The inevitable, foolish boasting of the enemy makes Yahweh stop just short of annihilating Israel (vv. 26-27). The people's return to nothingness would signal to the nations Yahweh's inability to protect his own. The fate of the people reflects the power of the god.

In vv. 28-33, Moses reports the divine judgment upon the nameless nation used as the instrument of the Lord's anger. That nation was too foolish to understand that its defeat of Israel was due not to its own superiority but to Yahweh's abandonment of Israel (vv. 30-31). The origin of the enemy nation (pictured as a vine) is from Sodom and Gomorrah, two cities proverbial for their wickedness (Gen 19). Israel, in contrast, is rooted in the rich land of Canaan and is full of the lifegiving power of the Lord (vv. 13-14).

Earlier in the poem Yahweh punished the sinful Israelites, immediately sending against them the curse of a "no people" (vv. 19-25). Verses 34-35 depict Yahweh as waiting before punishing the enemy nation which has through folly exceeded its role as instrument. Other biblical texts say of the divine delay in punishment that the guilty ones have not yet filled up the measure of their sins, i.e., the sins have not yet reached the point where punishment is decreed (vv. 34-35). The divine act which will punish the enemy and rescue Israel lies in the future, when Israel's destitution will invite Yahweh's compassion (v. 36a).

The day of punishment-rescue is by that fact a day of judgment, when good and evil are made public and dealt with. *RSV* "vindicate" in v. 36a is really "judge." Verses 37-39 is the judicial process: the judge's questions to the defendant followed by the verdict. The verses are addressed to the enemy nation as well as to Israel, both of them culpably foolish in not recognizing Yahweh's work. They are asked where are the gods, the rock, in whom they trusted for victory. Those gods whom Israel (and the "no-people") fed with offerings of fat and wine to gain their favor and support do nothing in this hour of trial. Yahweh, in contrast, had fed Israel with rich food in the holy land in vv. 12-14. The true nature of the other gods having been demonstrated by their inability to help and protect in v. 38b, Yahweh reveals his own sole power in the world. The language, and indeed the scene are reminiscent of Second Isaiah (cf. Isa 41:4; 43:10-11, 13, 25; 51:12) where the nations and Israel are to recognize Yahweh's power in a trial scene. Repeating his claim to unique deity, Yahweh declares that all events in the world, both of punishment and of rescue, come from him. None can deliver out of his hand (v. 39b), a claim underscored by the silence of the gods under divine questioning (v. 38b).

Yahweh, demonstrating himself as the only power before all the nations, whets the lightning of his sword (so the Hebrew literally) to requite all his enemies (vv. 40-42). The portrayal of the divine warrior, his enemies lying slain at his feet, is offensive to modern taste, accustomed to a gentle and forebearing God. The picture however is frequent in the Old Testament. One must first of all note that in the ancient East the god imposed himself or herself upon the worshiper through acts of power—and power was dramatically shown on the battlefield. Thus Israel portrayed its God, the only powerful God, as a divine warrior. Second, the power of God is not capricious but at the service of justice, punishing the wicked and rescuing those who call upon him.

The great poem ends appropriately with an invitation to the nations of the world, who have just witnessed the day of judgment. They are to praise his people, whose prosperity demonstrates the presence of the Lord. Israel is the people in whom the nations can encounter the Lord. The poem has narrated how the Lord is present in Israel—in its formation, its punishment, and in its rescue and vindication.

The Song thus fits admirably into the Book of Deuteronomy and particularly into the scheme of the third sermon. The book holds before the reader or hearer the prospect of blessing or curse. The Song dramatizes the scenario of curses while holding open blessings beyond the curses. The third part of Deuteronomy speaks from the experience of the exile and in this context the Song promises punishment for Israel's unjust oppressors and rescue for Israel.

According to v. 44, Moses went and recited the Song to

Israel, a verse that continues directly the action of 31:22 where Moses wrote it down. The different sources of chap. 31 show up also in vv. 44-47. Verse 44 continues the special source of 31:11-22 in which the Song is to be a witness reminding Israel of its infidelity. Verses 45-47 seem to continue 31:24-29 which contain many Deuteronomic expressions. The seriousness of the words of the *law* for Israel is there inculcated. Though the Song is not mentioned in the verses, their very position framing the Song suggests what 31:16-22 + 32:44 explicity state: the Song is an authoritative interpretation of the law. As the Song makes clear by its depiction of curses followed by blessings, Israel's happiness hangs on observance. They must make their children understand it (v. 46). Verse 47 is a powerful statement of the ability of the law to give life in the land.

Verses 48-52 are a source not as yet encountered in Deuteronomy, the Priestly redactor (P). It is widely held that P is responsible for the final arrangement of the Tetrateuch (Genesis-Numbers) and that he lived in the sixth century during the exile. Concerning v. 49, Mount Nebo is an unknown peak in the mountain range on the east side of the Jordan opposite Jericho. From here Moses takes his last look over the land toward which he has been leading the people for the past forty years. Now he is to die and his death is expressly linked to his sin at Meribah narrated in Num 20:1-13 (P). Unlike Deut 1:32 which interprets Moses' exclusion as due to the people's sin rather than his own, P attributes his exclusion to his own sin. It is a sober lesson for Israel in exile.

Verses 48-52 repeat and expand Num 27:12-14. It is probable that P repeats the account here and provides additional material in chap. 34 in order to join the whole book of Deuteronomy to the earlier book of the tetrateuch.

THE FOURTH SPEECH.
33:1—34:12

The fourth and last section in the scheme imposed upon the Deuteronomic traditions by the final redactor, the second editor of the Deuteronomistic History (Dtr²), is the Blessing of the tribes and the account of the death of Moses. It is likely that the Priestly redactor (P) has added to the Book, already redacted in four parts as we know it, his account of the Lord's command to Moses to ascend Mount Nebo (32:48-52) and his version of the death of Moses from the epic source (34:1-12). Like Isaac in Genesis 27 and Jacob in Genesis 49, Moses on the occasion of his dying moments will exercise the privilege of the venerable leader and declare the fortunes of the tribes as he gazes upon the land on which they will dwell. In chap. 34 P sets off the Mosaic era of lawgiving from what follows by making a sharp distinction between Moses and Joshua, a distinction that is not emphasized in the previous chapters of Deuteronomy.

Section 1.
The Blessing of Moses
33:1-29

33 This is the blessing with which
　　Moses the man of God blessed the
children of Israel before his death. ²He
said,
　　"The LORD came from Sinai,
　　　and dawned from Seir upon us;

he shone forth from Mount Paran,
he came from the ten thousands of
    holy ones,
    with flaming fire at his right hand.
³Yea, he loved his people;
    all those consecrated to him were in
    his hands;
so they followed in thy steps,
    receiving direction from thee,
⁴when Moses commanded us a law,
    as a possession for the assembly of
    Jacob.
⁵Thus the LORD became king in Jesh-
    urun,
    when the heads of the people were
    gathered,
    all the tribes of Israel together.

²⁶"There is none like God, O Jesh-
    urun,
    who rides through the heavens to
    your help,
    and in his majesty through the skies.
²⁷The eternal God is your dwelling place,
    and underneath are the everlasting
    arms.
    And he thrust out the enemy before
    you,
    and said, Destroy.
²⁸So Israel dwelt in safety,
    the fountain of Jacob alone,
    in a land of grain and wine;
    yea, his heavens drop down dew.
²⁹Happy are you, O Israel! Who is like
    you,
    a people saved by the LORD,
    the shield of your help,
    and the sword of your triumph!
Your enemies shall come fawning to
    you;
    and you shall tread upon their high
    places.''

According to the chronology of Deuteronomy, Moses' sermons are given on the day of his death (see under 1:3). But it is only toward the end of the book that his death is specially emphasized, in 31:2, 14, 16, 27 and 32:48-52. The great leader on the eve of his death, blessing his people, is familiar in the Bible. In Genesis 27 Isaac gives a deathbed blessing to Jacob and Esau. In Genesis 49, a text similar to Deuteronomy 33, Jacob calls his twelve sons together "that I may tell you what shall befall in days to come" (49:1). The future of each tribe is described allusively, possibly drawing upon popular traditions. The collection of traditions is described thus in Genesis: "This is what their father said to them as he blessed them, blessing each with a blessing suitable to him" (Gen 49:28). When God blesses man and woman, God enhances their life, increasing their fame, fortune, and progeny. When man and woman bless God or God's work, they acknowledge God's blessing by narrating the modes of God's enhancement of their life. The impending deaths of the patriarchs and of Moses gives them special insight into the future of their people. They describe that future and their narration itself is the blessing. In later biblical tradition the departing leader leaves a testament, not a blessing, that will continue his work— Joshua in Joshua 23 and Samuel in 1 Samuel 12. In the New Testament the testament tradition is found in the Last Discourse of Jesus in John 14-17.

In Deuteronomy 33 the blessings are framed by an ancient poem, vv. 1-5 and vv. 26-29. This poem describes Yahweh's march of conquest from his mountain Sinai with his heavenly army to "thrust out the enemy" (v. 27) from the land so that Israel might settle in safety. The same drama is described in other ancient poems, Judg 5:4-5, Ps 68:7-18, and Habakkuk 3. Unfortunately this ancient poetry is imperfectly preserved and understood. Certitude in translation therefore is often impossible.

The central action of the poem of vv. 1-5 + 26-29 is clear even if some details are obscure. Israel, like its neighbors, thought of its God Yahweh as dwelling on a mountain. He was seen as a storm deity manifesting himself in the storm;

thunder, lightning, strong wind were his weapons and his means of communication (cf. Ps 29). The high gods were often portrayed with a retinue of lesser gods fighting as allies. This Israelite poem retains the retinue but subordinates the heavenly figures to the point where their personalities virtually disappear. The storm theophany of vv. 1-5 effects victory and proclaims his kingship with the promulgation of his decrees (his "law," correcting v. 4 to "a law he gave us").

Yahweh's military might, visible in the storm, conquers the land for his people. That manifestation of might elicits the confession that there is no other deity except Yahweh, "there is none like the God of Jeshurun" (v. 26). Israel can enjoy the luxuriant fertility of the land now theirs (v. 28). Even their enemies recognize that the only powerful God is Israel's protector (v. 29).

Within the framework of the old poem describing the Lord's granting Israel their land, the blessings of the tribes are set. The context, which after all is the primary interpreter of any text, suggests that Israel's tribes receive their blessings in and through the land, an idea found throughout the entire book of Deuteronomy.

From a general survey of the whole, we turn to some of the details. Verses 1-5 describe Yahweh coming forth from his residence on Sinai, a mountain which in other ancient poems is in parallelism to Seir and Mount Paran. Since these latter sites are known to be directly south of the land of Canaan, many scholars are inclined to place Mount Sinai in the same southern area. The traditional identification of Mount Sinai with Jebel Musa (Arabic "Mount of Moses") in the Sinai Peninsula is late, attested only from the fourth century A.D. The verses begin the journey at Sinai, assuming that Yahweh has already rescued Israel from Egypt and brought them to his holy mountain. Now he is to accompany them in their conquest of the land with his army. "Shone forth" in v. 2 is a common term for God's appearance in a storm. The end of v. 2 should probably read: "And with his myriads of holy ones, At his right hand warriors of the gods, Yea, the purified ones of the peoples. All the holy ones are at thy hand. . . .'' Verses 2b and 3 describe the heavenly army, though the text is obscure. Verse 4 is probably to be read, ''A law he gave to us, a possession for the congregation of Jacob.'' The word ''Moses'' seems to be a copyists' error. The meaning apparently is that the Lord utters his decrees in the storm. The thunder is his royal voice, decreeing that he is king over the world and over his people, the latter represented by the heads of his people gathered for worship (v. 5). ''Jeshuran'' is a name for Israel, perhaps meaning ''pleasing (to God),'' hence ''friend,'' ''favorite.'' This condensed scene illustrates the dynamic character of kingship among the gods. A god establishes kingship by an awesome display of power especially of a military kind.

Reuben in v. 6 is the first of the twelve tribes to be blessed. Ephraim and Manasseh, the tribes of Joseph, are counted as two in v. 17 to bring the number to twelve. In Gen. 29:31—30:24 + 35:16-18 the birth of the twelve sons of Jacob are narrated in the following order, with the names of their mothers.

Leah	Reuben Simeon Levi Judah	*Bilhah*	Dan Naphtali	*Zilpah*	Gad Asher

Leah	Issachar Zebulon	*Rachel*	Joseph Benjamin

This exact order is followed neither in Genesis 49 nor in our chapter. The number apparently was fixed at twelve but some variety in the names and in the order was permitted.

It is known that the tribe of Reuben, settled in the east bank in northern Moab (Deut 3:12), disappeared from the record rather early, its territory thereafter being attributed to Gad. The blessing may be an allusive description of Reuben's tenuous existence despite his first born status entitling him to rank over his brothers. Gen 49:3-4 likewise restricts the blessing given to Reuben; he is not to have the first born's preeminence because he defiled his father's bed (Gen 35:22).

The blessing upon Judah is really a prayer that the Lord aid Judah who is in danger of being cut off from the tribal union because of military pressure upon it. The reference may be to Philistine encroachments in the twelfth-eleventh centuries.

Levi was the priestly tribe which was given no proper grant of land, being dependent upon the offerings of the other tribes for support (Deut 10:8-9; Num 1:47-54; Exod 32:25-29). Moses prays that Thummim and Urim (two sacred lots, one for "no" and the other for "yes," cast by the priest in response to petitioners' requests) be given into their charge (v. 8a). If the reference in v. 8b is to the Pentateuch as we have it today, then Levi must refer to the preeminent Levite, Moses, who was "tested//striven with" at "Massah/Meribah" (Exod 17:1-7 and Num 20:2-13). "Testing" here means putting a person in such a situation where his true mettle will be revealed. The Levites come through the crisis with flying colors and as a result are consecrated to the Lord. Such crises leading to ordination are found in Exod 32:25-29 and Num 25:10-13. The elite remained faithful amid the infidelity of its blood relatives (v. 9). Exod 32:29 expresses concisely the consecration, "Today you have ordained yourselves for the service of the Lord, each one at the cost of his son and of his brother, that he may bestow a blessing upon this day." From the Lord they receive "ordinances" and "thy law" to teach the people. Despite a popular misconception Old Testament priests are not exclusively sacrificers of animals; especially in the pre-exilic period they give legal decisions *(torah)* and transmit traditional teaching.

Over Benjamin Moses pronounces the blessing of security that comes from nearness to the Lord (v. 12). There is a play on words: the beloved of the Lord *dwells* in safety because the Lord *dwells* "amid his slopes," a phrase which can also mean "in his bosom."

The long blessing upon Joseph, the largest and most prosperous tribe, centers upon his richness and power (vv. 13-17). The land on which Joseph lives is declared blessed by the Lord, the blessings arising from a series of paired elements of the world—heaven above and the deep below, sun and moon (the latter in place of *RSV* "months"), mountains and hills. Often in ancient accounts of creation fertile land emerged as the last element in a listing of cosmic pairs such as those in vv. 13-16. The primordial state could be described, as it is in Gen 1:2, "without form and void," i.e. incapable of supporting human life because it is dominated by chaotic forces. The list of pairs shows that the disordered forces have been put in order by the creator so that human life may emerge. "The best gifts of the earth and its fulness" in v. 16a is the result of divine activity. *"Earth"* in v. 16a refers back to v. 13a, "Blessed by the Lord is his *earth*" (*RSV* "land"). In the climax of v. 16b, the creation of the fertile land is declared ultimately to be from "the favor of him that tented on Sinai." *RSV* "that dwelt in the bush," has essentially the same meaning since the bush is the bush of Sinai where the Lord appeared to Moses (Exod 3:2-3, with a play on *seneh* "bush," and *Sinai*). Yahweh's favor has made Joseph's land fertile. May the fertility of the land touch also the people who live upon it (v. 16b). The primary effect of the power of creation upon Joseph will be to make him first among the nations. "Bull" in v. 17a is an honorable title for gods and noblemen, emphasizing their military prowess. "Horn" in the same verse is a concrete noun for brute strength, especially in battle. Thus equipped Joseph can butt the nations from his land (v. 17b). Fecundity and power characterize Joseph, accounting for his large population which make necessary the two sub-groups of Ephraim and Manasseh (v. 17c).

The Galilean tribes Zebulun and Issachar are spoken of together in vv. 18-19. Verse 19 is too uncertain to draw any historical conclusions. Zebulun is apparently a tribe known for trading, in contrast to Issachar known for its sedentary life. "Sucking the affluence of the seas" may refer to wealth gathered in sea trade.

Gad was assigned land in Transjordan by Moses in Deut 3:12-17. Here in vv. 20-21 he is depicted as tough and warlike, choosing the best land for himself. The Hebrew text of v. 20a can easily be emended to "Blessed is the broad land of Gad," a translation more in accord with the rest of the blessing. The present text makes Yahweh the object of the blessing, unparalleled within the Blessing. Verse 21b seems out of place and may belong to v. 5, also a scene of gathered tribal heads and promulgation of law. As these textually uncertain verses now stand, they attribute to Gad a major role in lawgiving among the tribes.

The reference to Dan in v. 22 is mysterious since Dan has no known relation to the northern Transjordanian area of Bashan. At any rate, he is portrayed with the alert strength of a lion.

Naphtali in v. 23, enjoying the favor of the Lord, is to expand to the south and to the west (rather than "lake" of *RSV*). A secure grip on the land is the desire of every tribe. Promise of expansion gives extra assurance that the desire will be satisfied.

The north coast tribe of Asher is blessed, in vv. 24-25, with tribal unity ("let him be the favorite of his brothers"), with fertility ("let him dip his foot in oil"), and with the ability to defend himself. The last wish is expressed in concrete terms, doorbolts of iron and bronze. Verse 25b is uncertain.

Verses 26-29, as suggested already under vv. 1-5, is the closing half of the framing poem. The two parts of the single poem on the Lord's march of conquest from Sinai to Canaan frame the blessings and place them all under the gracious power of the Lord. The victory of Yahweh often elicited a cry "there is no god like you" from the dwellers of heaven and earth (cf. Exod 15:11 and Ps 89:8). The rest of v. 26 needs correction, "who rides through the heavens in might, who rides gloriously in majesty." Yahweh is a God who fights using the weapons of storm, "the (storm-)cloud rider." Verse 27 describes a scene like that of 32:10-11: Israel is found in danger of extinction and Yahweh, like a great bird, carries them to safety on his mighty wings. Like the poem of 32:10-14, the rescue of Israel is complete only with their safe dwelling in the land. According to the text, Israel cooperates with Yahweh in clearing out the enemy from the land, obeying the divine command, "Destroy!" (v. 27b). The poem ends with Israel secure in its rich land (v. 28). Verse 29 declares happy the people so saved and in possession of a fertile land. The Lord is their shield and sword preventing loss of the land. Their enemies see Israel's superiority by reason of their Lord's invincibility. They come to the land and do obeisance with the traditional gestures of vassals—allowing their master to place his foot on their neck or back. The last verse in *RSV* should be corrected, "You shall tread upon their backs."

A memorable picture! Moses, gifted with insight into Israel's future, declares the varying fortunes of the tribes under their Lord as they live in the land.

Section 2.
The Death of Moses
34:1-12

34 And Moses went up from the plains of Moab to Mount Nebo, to the top of Pisgah, which is opposite Jericho. And the Lord showed him all the land,

⁵So Moses the servant of the Lord died there in the land of Moab, according to the word of the Lord, ⁶and he buried him in the valley in the land of Moab opposite Beth-peor; but no man knows the place of his burial to

> this day. [7]Moses was a hundred and twenty years old when he died; his eye was not dim, nor his natural force abated.

The entire chapter, like the whole of Genesis-Numbers, has been edited by the Priestly redactor (P). P has selected old epic material (J-E) on the death of Moses and reshaped it in typical fashion, underscoring links to his own material in Genesis-Numbers by adding such phrases as "from the plains of Moab to Mount Nebo" in v. 1 and supplying chronology in v. 7. As suggested in the introduction, it is probable that chap. 34 or a version of it originally was the last chapter of the tetrateuch. It was then transferred to become the ending of Deuteronomy in order to attach Deuteronomy to the preceding books as their final statement, and no longer to stand as the preface to the Deuteronomistic History.

According to the text Moses ascends the mountain to the top of Pisgah which, to judge from 3:27, is an alternate designation of Mount Nebo. The plains of Moab is the low plain just north of the Dead Sea, in mass about nine miles north-south and six miles east-west. To the west is the Mishor or tableland, about 3500 feet above sea level, which slopes down to the low plain by way of irregular mountain ridges and summits. One of the summits on the western side of the Mishor is Mount Nebo, the top of Pisgah.

The Lord shows Moses the whole land, beginning in the north and then following a counter-clockwise direction (vv. 1b-3). The Western Sea is the Mediterranean. The Negeb is the southern part of Canaan. The Plain is the low plain on the west side of the Jordan corresponding to the plains of Moab. The mention of Zoah at the southern end of the Dead Sea suggests that for the author the Plain included both the northern and southern ends of the Sea.

The land that Moses sees is that promised to Abraham, Isaac, and Jacob. Israel will have to take it under Joshua but it is already theirs by divine word (v. 4). Moses dies, in death as in life entirely at the disposition of the divine word

(v. 5). His burial place is unknown (v. 6). His monument, more lasting than bronze, is the law which he mediates to all generations (vv. 6-8). He lives on too in Joshua and all who exercise the Mosaic function, "full of the spirit of wisdom" (v. 9), i.e., the ability to govern in the name of the Lord. But there never has been nor will there ever be a prophet like Moses, great because of the Lord's knowledge of him rather than because of his knowledge of God. The last three verses (vv. 10-12) are a theological reflection upon Moses and upon his work. Moses was renowned because the Lord chose him and equipped him to free Israel from bondage to Pharaoh and to demonstrate the unique power of the Lord to all Israel.

EXCURSUS ON LAW AND COVENANT

Israel, like any ancient Near Eastern nation, had a system of laws and made treaties, or covenants, to define important religious and secular transactions. Though Israel employed the same legal institutions as its Near Eastern neighbors, it had a distinctive perspective on law and covenant. Several factors made Israel different. *First,* Israel believed that its God, Yahweh, was the only powerful deity, and consequently made an exclusive claim upon its loyalty. Israel's law codes uphold exclusive service of Yahweh which distinguishes them from other codes. *Second* Israel alone had a consistent and ancient tradition forbidding images, which had important consequences for its view of the words of the law. "You shall have no other gods before me. You shall not make for yourself a graven image, or any likeness of anything that is in heaven above, or that is on the earth beneath, or that is in the water under the earth" (Deut 5:7-8). Since the customary image to reflect the deity's presence to the worshiper was forbidden, the people turned instead to the revealed word, there to encounter the Lord. "Then [at Sinai] the Lord spoke to you out of the midst of the fire; you heard the sound of words, but saw no form; there was only a voice" (Deut 4:12). The words of the law became intensely revelatory for the Israelite, denied other modes of divine-human encounter.

The *third* distinguishing mark was Israel's combining of its legal tradition with the covenant formulary to produce a genre without parallel—the speech of Moses.

Israel's perspective on law and covenant has to be seen against the background of the theory and practice of its neighbors. Ancient Near Eastern law differs from modern law by its religious basis. The gods who created the world established orders within the world which are just. Laws regulated the behavior of men and women, and looked especially to the righting of the divinely implanted justice that had been violated by human transgression. The king, as the servant of the god, was the overseer of justice, and played an important role in administering the law. On the famous law code of Hammurabi the Great of Babylon (1728-1686 B.C.), the upper half of the stele pictures the king receiving the entire code from the god Shamash. Mesopotamian codes are promulgated by kings to display themselves as faithful upholders of the justice which the gods implanted in the world. The code, then, is primarily a statement of the divine order and the king's role in it, rather than the record of the legal practice of the age. One is therefore not surprised at the discrepancy between the laws of the codes and actual practice as evidenced in legal documents.

Israelite law was remarkably similar in style and often in substance with the Mesopotamian evidence, though admittedly evidence for the everyday practice of law is lacking. In the Covenant Code (Exod 20:22—23:33), for instance, one finds the casuistic form common in the Hammurabi Code: "If a man steals an ox or a sheep, and kills it or sells it, he shall pay five oxen for an ox, and four sheep for a sheep," etc. (Exod 22:1). If the Mesopotamian codes were primarily statements of divine justice and royal duty, the Israelite codes are probably to be interpreted in the same way. They defined divine justice for Israel. They do not necessarily record day-to-day legal custom.

Beside casuistic law, apodictic law in the second-person is found in the Israelite codes. An apodictic law is a prohibition, prescription, instruction, frequently but not always in the second-person, enjoining or forbidding a certain activity without stating a penalty, e.g., "You shall not revile God, nor curse a ruler of your people" (Exod 22:28). Such admonitions are not found in the Mesopotamian codes but are found elsewhere in rituals and in some Hittite vassal treaties where exhortation is part of the genre. Because the Israelite codes are really speeches of Moses, the wide use of the apodictic form is not surprising.

Covenant is one of the instruments of ancient Near Eastern law. For the sake of clarity, some authors use "treaty" for extra-biblical agreements, and "covenant" for the biblical phenomenon. The ancient Near East has been well described as "a society of gentlemen" where virtually all important agreements were sworn in oaths. That a person is as good as his word is an important principle in an honor-shame society such as those of the ancient East. "May the gods do such and such to me if I do not do to you as I have sworn today in their presence!" would be a typical formula. The ancient practice bears some resemblance to business practice in small towns, just a few decades ago, when important decisions were often oral, sealed by a handshake, and sanctioned by the businessman's fear of losing his reputation in his community.

Certain kinds of treaties were written down, especially treaties between kings designed to set policy for many generations. These treaties were more elaborate than the simple statement of obligations and divine witnesses that made up the treaties of daily commerce. (The outline of a complex state treaty can be seen in the Introduction.) Written documents recording Hittite, Syrian, and Assyrian treaties are extant, all attesting to a common pattern that admitted of variety.

In the 1950's several scholars pointed out the similarities between the covenant formularies in use in the Hittite Empire (1450-1200 B.C.) and the Mosaic covenant. They proposed that borrowing had taken place. Yahweh was the suzerain who graciously made Israel his vassal, imposed his law, or stipulations, and placed before the people blessings and curses. As attractive as the impulse is to find evidence of the covenant formulary in the Mosaic period (usually understood as the thirteenth century B.C.), the wiser course is to follow such cautious specialists as Dennis Mc-Carthy who see the Deuteronomic central discourse of 4:44—26:68 as the first self-conscious and full scale adaptation by Israel of the covenant formulary. The Mosaic, and even the patriarchal covenants, were of course true covenants. In "a society of gentlemen" such important transactions could not but be covenants. But the adaptation of the specialized covenant formulary is the contribution of the Deuteronomist. One can also admit that the mature formulation of Deuteronomy had forerunners, "pre-Deuteronomic" speeches such as 1 Samuel 12 and Joshua 24.

Several lines of evidence support the view that Deuteronomy was the first articulator of the coherent covenant theology. To assert that Moses borrowed the Hittite covenant pattern raises unanswerable questions of how the Israelites of the thirteenth century B.C. could have known them with such thoroughness as to shape their self-understanding within these Hittite categories. Even assuming that the Hittite formulary had been borrowed by Israel, why is not the formulary, so suitable for rebuke, a staple of the preaching of the pre-exilic prophets? And can one really see the Hittite formulary operative *as a pattern* outside Deuteronomy?

A more attractive hypothesis than the hypothesis of Hittite origin is that Israel made use of the covenant formulary in its first millennium guise, exemplified by the Neo-Assyrians. Recently published examples of Neo-Assyrian versions, and fresh study of Assyrian treaty terminology, suggest that the Neo-Assyrians borrowed the West-Semitic formulary to deal with its western vassals. Israel would thus have been familiar with what, after all, was a West-Semitic instrument of international law.

A likely time for Israel's adaptation of the formulary is the second half of the eighth century, when it had to face for the first time in its history a superpower completely beyond its strength. In 743 B.C. Tiglathpileser III made the first of his western campaigns. His successors continued his policy of expansion, and of using the covenant formulary as an instrument of that expansion. The time was ripe for Israel to define its loyalties afresh, to reappropriate its classic story of exodus-conquest in the light of the Assyrian crisis. Deut 4:44—28:68 cannot of course be reduced entirely to a response to a foreign king who attempted to enter into an agreement with Israel which made him its suzerain. The traditions were too fixed for that. But Judah, menaced by a superpower which had just annihilated its northern sister, Israel in 722 B.C., would naturally see itself again on the edge of the Promised Land, waiting to see whether the Lord would settle them safely in the land.

Israel therefore casts its old traditions into the form of the covenant formulary, so that Moses once again might address it on how to be faithful to its true suzerain in a time of crisis. The covenant formularies often began with a detailed record of the past relations of suzerain and vassal, emphasizing the suzerain's love and benefits. The suzerain could command fidelity and even love in that personalized world of politics. How much more impressive than any human suzerain's record is Yahweh's record of benefits, chiefly in the exodus-conquest, which actually gave being to Israel. With how much more right can he command love and the observance of all his stipulations.

As impressive as is Israel's transformation of the ancient institutions of law and covenant, its combining of them into the new genre of the speech of Moses is even more impressive. Their combination is concisely told in Deut 26:16-19. The translation and division into sense lines is borrowed from Dennis McCarthy.

> This day you have confirmed Yahweh's declaration that he will be your God,

and that you will walk in his ways,
and that you will observe his statutes and his commandments and his decisions,
and that you will hearken to his voice,
whereas he has confirmed your declaration
since you are ready to be made his people, a special
possession, as he promised you,
that you will keep his commandments, as he sets you
high over all the nations which he has made, in praise
and in fame and in glory,
and so to be a people holy to Yahweh your God, as he
promised.

Moses tells Israel that its statutes, commandments, and ordinances, i.e. its legal traditions, have become the stipulations of its covenant with Yahweh. The legal tradition
gains a new context which will forever interpret it. Israel
can now manifest fundamental and exclusive loyalty to its
covenant Lord by obedience to his statutes, ordinances,
and commandments. The multitude of commandments offer Israel new possibilities of encounter with the Lord, new
opportunities of manifesting fundamental loyalty through
the acts of daily life.

The effect of the Deuteronomic placement of the
stipulations of the law within the covenant is that the
words of the law now have an incomparable significance in
bringing Israel before the Lord. From this perspective, one
can well understand the fascination and reverence for the
law felt by Jews throughout the ages. The Christian will
differ from the Jew in believing that the person of Jesus
Christ is now the place of encounter with God and the
manifestation of divine love.

FURTHER READING

Commentaries:

S. R. Driver, *A Critical and Exegetical Commentary on Deuteronomy*. The International Critical Commentary (Edinburgh: T. & T. Clark, 1901).
Thorough, judicious, and clearly written, it remains the best commentary in any language.

G. von Rad, *Deuteronomy, A Commentary*. The Old Testament Library (Philadelphia: Westminster, 1966).
A theological commentary by the most influential writer on Deuteronomy until quite recently. Clear and insightful.

J. Blenkinsopp, "Deuteronomy," in *The Jerome Biblical Commentary* (Englewood Cliffs: Prentice-Hall, 1968), 101-122.
Concise commentary taking into account historical detail and theological concerns.

W. L. Moran, "Deuteronomy," in *A New Catholic Commentary on Holy Scripture* (London: Nelson, 1969), 256-76.
Concise commentary with emphasis on structure of the book and on the rhetoric of speeches. Account is also taken of the ancient Near Eastern context.

General works:

G. von Rad, "Deuteronomy," in *The Interpreter's Dictionary of the Bible* (New York: Abingdon, 1962) I, 831-38.
Interestingly written, comprehensive discussion of the book. Needs supplementation by Lohfink, below.

N. Lohfink, "Deuteronomy," in *The Interpreter's Dictionary of the Bible Supplementary Volume* (New York: Abingdon, 1976), 229-32. Perceptive update of von

Rad's article. Perhaps the clearest and briefest exposition of the promising new approaches to the book.

N. Lohfink, *Höre Israel Auslegung von Texten aus dem Buch Deuteronomium* (Dusseldorf: Patmos, 1965).
Extraordinary popularization of several chapters in Deuteronomy 5-11.

M. Weinfeld, *Deuteronomy and the Deuteronomic School* (Oxford: Clarendon, 1972).
Scholarly discussion of the Deuteronomic style and its use of the treaty form.

D. McCarthy, *Treaty and Covenant*. Analecta Biblica 21a. (Rome: Biblical Institute, 1978).
The most authoritative statement of the present state of discussion of Deuteronomy and ancient Near Eastern treaties.

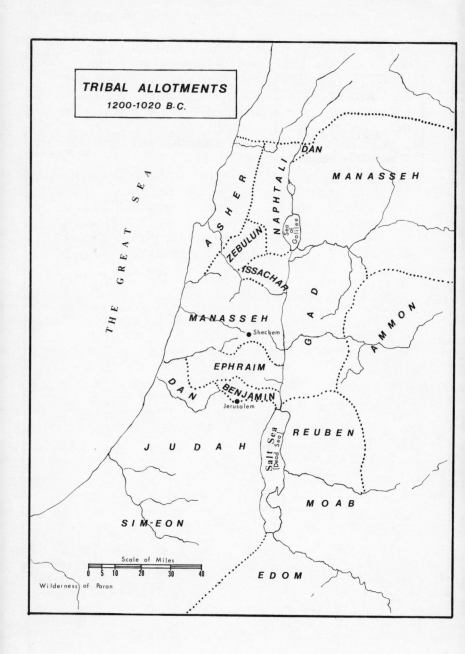

TRIBAL ALLOTMENTS
1200-1020 B.C.

THE GREAT SEA

ASHER

NAPHTALI

DAN

MANASSEH

ZEBULUN

Sea of Galilee

ISSACHAR

GAD

MANASSEH

Shechem

AMMON

EPHRAIM

DAN

BENJAMIN

Jerusalem

REUBEN

Salt Sea (Dead Sea)

JUDAH

MOAB

SIM-EON

Scale of Miles

0 5 10   20   30   40

Wilderness of Paran

EDOM

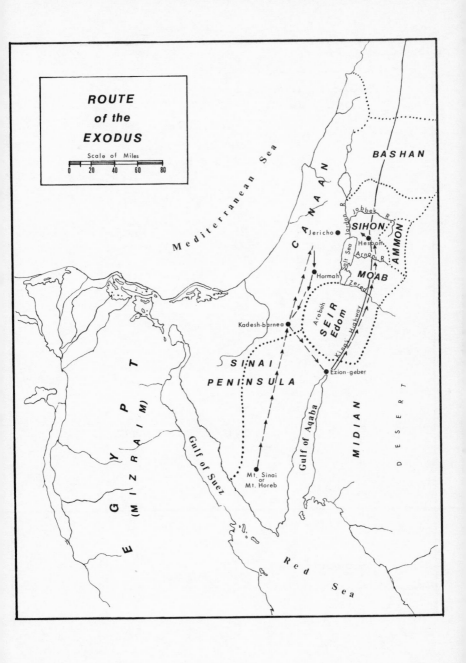

ROUTE
of the
EXODUS

Scale of Miles

0   20   40   60   80

Mediterranean Sea

BASHAN

C A N A A N

Jericho

SIHON

Heshbon

AMMON

Jabbek R

Dead Sea

Arnon R

Jordan R

MOAB

Hormah

Zered

Arabah

SEIR
Edom

King's Highway

Kadesh-barnea

SINAI

PENINSULA

Ezion-geber

MIDIAN

D E S E R T

E   G   Y   P   T

(M I Z R A I M)

Gulf of Suez

Gulf of Aqaba

Mt. Sinai
or
Mt. Horeb

Red   Sea

NEW TESTAMENT MESSAGE
A Biblical-Theological Commentary
Editors: Wilfrid Harrington, O.P. & Donald Senior, C.P.

Individual volumes may be purchased separately
• **22 Volume Set, cloth edition $198**   • **22 Volume Set, paperback $129**

GALILEE
From Alexander the Great to Hadrian
323 B.C.E. to 135 C.E.
by Sean Freyne

"It is a detailed, documented study that will probably be definitive on the subject."

Christianity Today

"His treatment is comprehensive, including chapters dealing *inter alia* with the geography of Galilee, the rise of Hellenism, Roman administration, the cities, social stratification, the attitude of Galilean Jewry towards the Jerusalem temple and halakhah, and the early development of Christianity."

Theological Studies

"The work is very thorough, fully documented, and a most valuable contribution to the study of early Judaism and early Christianity."

William Sanford LaSor, Fuller Theological Seminary

"The painstaking research, careful analyses, and cautious conclusions make it a model to follow for others similarly launching out into new territories. It will prove invaluable to New Testament scholars."

Christianity Today

Cloth $27.50